Praise for *The Ac*

'I have chuckled, I have belly laughed, I have shed tears. I loved this book! I love how Tim weaves words, like weaving a fine mat: bringing all the threads together to make a complete and vivid picture.

Tim's views on reading and "readiness" are so important. How many of our kids — and statistically often our Māori and Pasifika kids — have the label "failure" hanging around their necks and pulling them down by the time they are six? Many of the philosophies and beliefs Tim holds, in particular about Māori education and te reo Māori, are now argued for by ministries and government.'
Hoana Pearson QSM

'Tim Heath, motivated by educationalists Elwyn Richardson, Sylvia Ashton-Warner and Herbert Read, sets out as an "accidental teacher" with visions of bonding with his pupils and "wandering joyously through a trail of learning, laughter and mutual respect".

In this wonderfully engaging memoir, we are taken through the decades as Tim goes up against bureaucracy, fixed attitudes and ingrained Pākehā values, as well as resistance to his enthusiasm and ideals.

Throughout Tim's inspirational story is quiet evidence of the nourishment and understanding he provides for the children in his care. His protégés are encouraged to develop organically, like the plants he nurtures in the gardens around his schools. Art evolves intuitively, rather than being "taught" in a regimented way; his role as teacher is to set boundaries, supply materials and guidance, and then allow natural creativity to blossom. Similarly, reading usually flourishes when the child is ready, as long as the necessary ingredients and time are provided.

Along with all this, Tim puts in the unflinchingly hard work that both successful gardening and dedicated teaching entails.'
Judith White, novelist

'The journey Tim takes us on in *The Accidental Teacher* is a brave and courageous one. It's the story of an honest man with a big heart who cares for the downtrodden and not-so-privileged children. That includes my people – had I had him for a teacher I probably would have jumped at the opportunity to paint in the mornings and run around the grounds during class time.

Tim shares his aspiration to teach all children well, while giving them their due and honouring the mana they have as human beings – something that pre-Christian indigenous communities did naturally.'
Sharon Aroha Hawke, Ngāti Whātua Ōrakei

'By turns heartbreaking and funny, Tim's book describes a teaching practice that is personal and engaging. At times there are rules; at other times the rules can get stuffed. Every child, Tim argues, will benefit when all children are included.

Tim writes of a teaching life in which the values of connection, engagement and community formed the cornerstone.

The Accidental Teacher provides the inspiration for the kind of teaching that makes the classroom a place of practical dreams, and that's got to be good for everyone.'
Tony O'Brien, Associate Professor, Mental Health Nursing, University of Waikato

Tim Heath

The Accidental Teacher

The joys, ambitions, ideals, stuff-ups and heartaches of a teaching life

ALLEN&UNWIN
SYDNEY•MELBOURNE•AUCKLAND•LONDON

First published in 2021

Allen & Unwin
Level 2, 10 College Hill, Freemans Bay
Auckland 1011, New Zealand
Phone: (64 9) 377 3800
Email: auckland@allenandunwin.com
Web: www.allenandunwin.co.nz

83 Alexander Street
Crows Nest NSW 2065, Australia
Phone: (61 2) 8425 0100

A catalogue record for this book is available from
the National Library of New Zealand.

ISBN 978 1 98854 779 4

Design by Saskia Nicol
Set in Newsreader
Printed in Australia by McPherson's Printing Group

1 3 5 7 9 10 8 6 4 2

To nearly all teachers, everywhere

Contents

1.

THE S-TYPE BEDFORD was the number one truck. It was high, flat-fronted and had a unique, sometimes dreaded, 'forward control' system. This meant that the driver was seated ahead of the gear lever and had to reach backwards to change gear, to do the double declutch move we all thought so nifty.

It was 1961 and I was a student, with a duffle coat, a cherrywood pipe and a head full of attitudes. This was my second year as a 'holiday driver' for one of the city's largest cartage firms, and this summer I was a graduate, not from the university but from the more strenuous ranks of small truck driving. Graduated from the J and JA Bedfords to the S. This elevation in both status and driving position filled me with pride – quite undeserved in that I never totally mastered a forward-control gear change and did the occasional graunch, particularly when making the tricky change down from third to second. I continue, to this day, to double declutch whenever I am lucky enough to drive a manual vehicle. The procedure, to quote Google, is '. . . to change to a lower gear in a motor vehicle by first placing the gear lever into the neutral position before engaging the desired gear, at the same time releasing the clutch pedal and increasing the engine speed'. This skill, like so many, became redundant about forty, if not fifty, years ago, but it still impresses my grandchildren, especially those who are under ten.

My first year at university had been a success: I had passed the required three units, all with the C grade we saw as a reflection of good time management; played Second Grade rugby; had an emotive article extolling Fidel Castro published in the student magazine *Craccum*; and almost gained a girlfriend. I had taken, and passed, Social Anthropology Stage One. I had been told this was an easy option but had become fascinated by it. I especially enjoyed the tutorials with famed Professor Ralph Piddington in his dingy office with its leather chairs and dusty books. Along with his wisdom, the good professor would hand out peppermints for the ladies and cigarettes for the men. This was, I repeat, 1961.

I loved time in the café, arguing, drinking bad coffee, looking for issues to complain about. I heard two older students rubbishing my Castro article and was delighted that they had read it. Less delighted to see the potential girlfriend publicly involved in the physical activity she had, only a few days earlier, indicated to me she was not ready for. The fact that the recipient of her affections was a front-row prop from our team did not help.

We told each other that the caf, on a rainy day, smelt like a cow shed, even though none of us had been within ten miles of a cow, even on a fine day. We all laughed when the toilet-paper dispensers, with their inadequate and unpleasant shiny squares of paper, were engraved with the words 'BA's – Help Yourselves'. We were paid to be there. Some of us wore a tie. We warned each other against picking up the mortgage we were entitled to from the Housing Corporation before we were ready. We believed, once qualified, that a job awaited us. Not just a job, but the job we wanted, where we wanted. Did we know how lucky we were? No, we did not.

Despite all this good fortune, a holiday job was still needed. The three months off over Christmas and New Year was still firmly a 'holiday', not yet Americanised to 'vacation'. Young men headed, variously, to the freezing works, the wool stores and the trucks. Truck driving was the lowest paid, but by far the most pleasant, not least because there was usually a long waiting time before the right machine could be found to unload an item too heavy to move by hand. One year the shortage of cranes and fork hoists allowed me to read all four volumes of Lawrence Durrell's *Alexandria Quartet*. Even today, I associate this great work with reading in the hot cab of a truck, being dirty and fending off accusations of snobbery from fellow drivers.

There were other loads to be picked up from the wharves – hessian bags from South Africa containing a strange, furry brown rock that scratched the inside of our arms and produced an unpleasant dust; sacks of plaster each one hundredweight, if I remember rightly; and huge cartons of cigarettes. Once, when I was about to comment on how easy one of these boxes was to lift, I received a stare from the rheumy eye of a tally clerk. When I became a teacher, I tried to emulate this look but lacked the necessary economic motivation.

We, the motley, inept students, were wanted. These were times of full employment, times when bosses wanted their long-term workers to be able to go on holiday with their families. The prime minister, 'Kiwi Keith' Holyoake, spoke of the value of the family, and the country's economy was such that it seemed like families were valued, that families could have homes and a decent life, that students could have free education. These were golden years. My friends and I mocked Sir Keith and called him by his second name, Jacka, whenever we remembered.

My chief delight in the driving job was getting to know the other drivers. I had met many of them the previous year. I was looked upon as a student, an outsider, a reader of books, but I had established that I was willing to do my share of the work and to buy a round when it was my turn. You are observed when you are involved in physical labour – do you pick up the bag of cement from the top of the pile or grab your share of the ones at the bottom? Do you fetch a broom when it's needed? Do you join the union?

Ticks were given out grudgingly, but I had earned enough to be part of a group that raced to the now-defunct Astor Hotel at the end of the day. Six o'clock closing, and 'race' was the key word – even now, sixty years later, I still drink beer too quickly. The Astor was my downfall. I couldn't keep pace with my mates. They were seasoned drinkers; I was an eighteen-year-old student who legally should not have been there. They could buy ten jugs at five to six and have them empty by ten past. I thought this was a glorious achievement.

Many of my fellow drivers – love that phrase – were Māori in the city for the first time, part of a much-written-about 'urban drift'. There was also an increasing number of workers from Sāmoa, Tonga, Niue and Rarotonga – all lumped together as Pacific Islanders and called by a series of derogatory terms. I found it exciting to meet these men. They represented something different, something new. Some of my early childhood and first school years had been spent in the Northland town of Kaikohe, where I grew up believing Māori and Pākehā were separate, apart. There were separate schools, separate churches, and separate days to pick up the Family Benefit payments from the Post Office. At the Saturday afternoon pictures, Māori sat downstairs, Pākehā sat upstairs. After Kaikohe, my family went to Howick in east Auckland. Howick had been founded as a fortress town, designed to defend settlers from marauding Māori. Suffice it to say I encountered very few Māori there in my primary school years.

MY MEMORIES OF primary school are not so much vague as bitsy. Some scenes are as strong today as they ever were, but most have drifted away in a blur of the happy and the not so happy. Two of these 'as clear as if it happened yesterday' experiences are worth describing in some detail, though there are other strong contenders, like having a fist fight with another boy while a hundred chanting kids danced around us, egging us on, wanting it to get worse. I got the strap afterwards, to teach me not to be violent.

The first of these memories is of learning to read. I was

seven, nearly eight, and my parents and my teachers were worried. In Primer Four when I came to the front of the long queue of kids waiting, with ragged reading books dangling from listless hands, for the teacher to hear us read, I would start boldly with a memorised passage and then run out. The teacher would get angry and slap my legs, convinced I was pretending. 'If you can read that much you can read more. You are just being lazy/silly/naughty/wasting my time and I shall talk to your father — I know him and we both know he won't be pleased.' My parents were more enlightened and there were no random leg slaps, although if things got too bad there was a formal session in the washhouse with the wooden spoon.

The truth was, I didn't know what they were all on about. I loved it when my father read to us, but the notion that the marks on the page had some connection to the stories eluded me. My teacher would make sounds, looking like a pantomime clown, and we would copy her, eyes rolling and mouths rigid with suppressed laughter. She would then write a word on the blackboard, take us through the sounds and marvel at our inability to see the whole. To this day, I believe phonics only really works for people who already know how to read.

Then, one day, I got it. Everything fell into place. I raced through the readers in their neat boxes, then picked up one of the *School Journals* reserved for the best readers, all of them girls.

'What are you doing with that journal, Timothy Heath!' my teacher bellowed.

'Reading it, Miss. Story about men crossing big mountains.'

'Come here and read it to me then. If you can't, I am going to punish you for putting your dirty little hands on the girls' special books.'

I read it to her, using my father's expression and accuracy. I wanted to read more, but she stood up and raced out of the room. I like to think she had wet her pants but have no proof.

I was subsequently reprimanded by the headmaster, and my father, for wasting everybody's time by pretending not to be able to read for all those years. There was no praise, no belief that it had happened all of a rush, and no understanding of the joy that being able to read had given me, of my feeling of freedom. I would, however, be asked to read passages from the *New Zealand Herald* to my parents' friends. I still had to chop the kindling, help weed the garden and do my share of the dishes, but I sensed things had changed, that I was no longer a worry.

I remember many of my classmates, but the one who comes to mind most vividly is Max. Max, the boy who couldn't. He was amiable, generous, kind and humorous, but incapable of understanding the stuff that went on in the classroom. We were all scared of our teacher, Mrs Rudkin, but Max, who had the most to fear, just seemed resigned to her regime. Mrs Rudkin believed she was a great teacher and if children didn't learn from her words of wisdom they deserved to be beaten. We all had moments when fear, or ignorance, meant the ten spelling words we had learned the night before had somehow disappeared. She had a round wooden ruler that instilled learning via blows to the knuckles. It was regrettable that the daily spelling test was followed by handwriting. We knew handwriting was a sacred activity and errors were blasphemy, but smarting knuckles made it impossible to hold a pen correctly, and sin was inevitable. Sometimes she didn't see your work as she prowled around the room and you had a lucky escape. She always saw Max's work, and we would flinch to see him being punished again. I wanted to say, 'He's dumb, he doesn't understand, Miss.' But I never did. All I did do was take the memory of Max into my teaching, and never punished kids for not knowing, apart from the slow punishment of giving so much more time and praise to those who succeeded. The cynical adage 'to those that have, more shall be given' prevails in every classroom.

My parents sent me to King's College, a private Anglican school that regarded itself as the most prestigious in the country. I am not totally sure why this decision was made. My brother went to Auckland Grammar, which regarded itself as the most prestigious state school in the country. This was one of many confusions in my upbringing – too many to be dealt with here. Suffice it to say that my father was an Anglican vicar and King's College reduced fees by 66 per cent for the sons of vicars.

There were no Māori or Pasifika students to be encountered at King's. This was long before rugby scholarships made their dramatic impact on schools, communities, sports competitions and, more importantly, individuals. In my final year at school, adolescent stirrings and the state of the world started to dawn on me. I would carry around my books with my largely unread airmail copy of the *New Statesman* draped as visibly as possible over the top. I was editor of the school magazine and wrote an editorial about how the school roll did not reflect the population of the country, how the only Māori we saw were those working in domestic roles in the school kitchen and laundry. I wrote of how I wanted this to change, wanted Māori and Pasifika students in my class. It is true that senior students from Queen Victoria School for Māori Girls came for an annual afternoon tea, but there were strict measures put in place to prevent any serious getting-to-know-you activities. The attitude towards these girls was patronising; staff commented on their cleanliness and excellence of speech; that we should learn their language was unthinkable. Needless to say, my editorial was censored, and I was instructed to write of glorious sporting achievements. I was delighted to have a real issue to fight, but the final editorial was an ugly amalgamation of cross-cultural and cross-kicking understanding.

King's College embodied many things I came to despise as a teacher – privilege, hierarchy, exam orientation, mono-culturalism, corporal punishment, ambiguous adherence to religious belief and Anglophilia. We had several hours of military drill on Monday afternoons with a master who transformed himself once a week, or twice if need be, into a major-general. In my final year I declared myself to be a conscientious objector. Much to my dismay, the school was very understanding, and I was told to take myself to the library, read my communist newspaper and not talk about my beliefs to younger pupils. Denied the stage I so dearly sought, I felt a strange isolation as I heard the school band, strong on rhythm, weak on tune, strike up a Sousa march, off-key and loud, inspiring the boys to march around the Number One rugby field in a slightly agricultural manner, trying to ignore the intimate scratching of khaki serge uniforms and the weight of World War One SMLE .303 rifles. I remembered how we would wait, breathless, when the required circuit was finished, and listen to the major-general's shrill voice utter the words that we would later use with our friends in a wide variety of contexts, not all of them seemly: 'That was good, but it was not good enough!' So, we would march again, hoping we could overcome the stumble and stutter of the band. I missed the agony of it all and, after a few weeks, sought permission to return to my role as corporal. Permission was granted, but I was instructed that any further subversion would be punished.

We attended chapel every morning. There were hymns, prayers and a Bible reading. We all sang with gusto and some accuracy, although most Third Formers exercised restraint, fearing their voices would make unexpected leaps from boyish soprano to masculine bray. We were expected to be 'men of faith'. I tried to be, but we had been taken to Eden Park to sit on the sideline and watch the immortal Fourth Test between the All Blacks and the dreaded Springboks. For several years, my theological thoughts were confused — I had elevated Kevin Skinner, Tiny White and Peter Jones to a special Trinity, more easily revered than the one offered in chapel. This sporting pantheon increased after we, again on the sideline of Eden Park, watched the last day of the cricket test match between New Zealand and the West Indies. This was New Zealand's first ever test victory and I was there.

Inevitably, I elevated John Reid to my pantheon. No wonder I went on to play club cricket, in a moderately unsuccessful way, until I was sixty-five.

Despite all the things about the school that I despised, then and now, I loved the place, and my five years there were, as they say, among the best of my life. I loved the sports, the music, the oak trees that lined the drive, and the library. The headmaster was one of the most influential people in my life.

We were all caned and it is hard to see how universal punishment could influence individual behaviour – you were a misfit if you *weren't* caned. On one occasion the end of the cane hit the ping-pong ball in my pocket; neither the master nor I knew which one of us had been shot. Sports were always available and always demanded everything we could give. Besides rugby and cricket, I involved myself in boxing, a sport in which I seemed to come second more often than I wished.

The music master, Mr L C M Saunders, remains a hero, a demi-god. He, built like a front-row forward, would stand on the stage of the school theatre, sleeves rolled up, and confront his audience of about eighty teenage boys. He would tell us the stories of the great operas, using a mixture of LP records, his own singing and piano playing. We had to sing Verdi choruses with him, hum Puccini and be as loudly Wagnerian as we could manage.

I was enthralled and spellbound. I don't know if everyone else was, but none of us disturbed the man's brilliant, virtuosic teaching. I am still grateful that he introduced me to jazz, and especially to the sadly neglected 1943 musical *Carmen Jones*. Music from the 'proper' opera of that name is played remarkably often on the Concert Programme; each time I hear it, I find myself singing along with the musical's slick lyrics. Every year he trained the whole school to sing, with a little help from his friends, Handel's 'Messiah' and Bach's 'St Matthew Passion'. And then there was a light musical opera. I kid you not. Did I mention he was also, for many years, esteemed music critic for the *New Zealand Herald*? If I managed to influence any of my students as deeply and positively as he influenced me, I shall die happy.

The headmaster was Mr G N T Greenbank, a man of mana and charisma, a man who truly arrived before he got there. He was much feared, and old boys will still tell you tales of injustice and fiery temper, of eccentricity, of how quadratic equations can be understood once you see their relationship to a Taranaki gate. He, at a time when the world confused me, became my friend. In my Third Form year I was with a group in the wrong place at the wrong time – it was easy to be in the wrong place in a school where patches of grass were deemed to be sacrosanct for no obvious reason. The others fled, but I stayed. I don't know whether this was defiance or whether I was rooted to the spot by fear. I was punished, as one must be, but he took note of me, praised me for not running away, watched me, lauded my progress, and spent many hours talking to me about literature, music, spirituality and the next First XV game. I was not alone in having him as a confidant and mentor – I, and many others, still wonder how he found the time and the strength to run a demanding school and still be able to give so much to individuals. Indeed one of the great men.

Another great man was my Latin teacher, Mr R B Sibson.

He could explain everything about the language except why we were learning it. His main love, however, was not teaching, or Latin, but birds. At one memorable school assembly, the headmaster, with a mixture of amusement and frustration, announced: 'Men, we sent your library master, Mr R B Sibson, to the city to spend this year's library budget.'

The school was in Middlemore, and you could catch a train to Central Auckland — a train to the city, as so many characters in English novels did. It needs also to be noted that we were called 'Men', however young and spotty we were. Everyone was called by their initials — I have friends today whom I still call, god help me, JWK and AW.

The headmaster continued. 'Mr R B Sibson came back, Men, with one book. Do not look on the library shelves for rows of new literature, for a new encyclopaedia to extend your minds. This year there is but one new book!'

With a flourish, and what we took to be a grin, he waved the original copy of Buller's *A History of the Birds of New Zealand* that Mr R B Sibson had been unable to resist. We did not know whether to laugh or express shock. When the book was handed back to him with a pantomime of care such as would be given to a baby, and received with gentle embrace, we realised that laughter was called for.

The book would now be worth many times the 1958 library budget, but the financial astuteness of the purchase was not perceived at the time. Every time I visit the Pukorokoro Miranda Shore Bird Centre, it gives me great pleasure to see the name 'R B Sibson' inscribed over the door to the main room. A fitting tribute to a true enthusiast.

IN FEBRUARY 1962, the truck-driving holiday was drawing to an end and the start of the university year loomed. This caused me hours of deep thought, not because I had any doubts about continuing with my degree, but because I had spent all my wages on the social side of truck driving. Most of it had been passed over the bar at the Astor Hotel. This hotel, incidentally, was on the busy corner of Symonds Street and Khyber Pass Road. In the 1980s it was demolished so that cars making a left-hand turn towards the motorway could move more quickly — I mourned the loss of this scene of so much of my growing up. Never again would I gaze upon its purple carpet full of whirls, crescents and spilt beer. Never again would I see Driver Smith coming to our table with two jugs, a huge grin and an untucked shirt, oblivious to the clock that said five past six. If people were to ask me where some of the most important formative experiences of my life took place, I would have to point out a busy corner of a road full of cars moving with indecent haste.

I sat talking to my brother's girlfriend about my dilemma. I adored her. I tended to adore every girl who sat and talked with me. I adored her name, Deanna Tamborini, her dark eyes and the way she held my hands when the conversation became serious. This conversation was serious, and I admit trying to make it really, really serious. I couldn't get through the university year on the student Bursary alone. No one else was going to chip in to see me through, especially my parents, who felt they had contributed enough to my education, who had seen me stagger home and go straight to sleep, who thought my new friends were not a good idea, especially as they had met so many polite, well-spoken young chaps from my school.

'You could,' Deanna said, looking into my eyes, 'you could go to teachers' college.'

I was shocked. Like the little tugboat, I was meant for bigger things.

She explained that if I passed three units, part-time, while at teachers' college I could be awarded a full-time year, on full pay, to complete my degree. This was starting to sound interesting, as was the thought that it might be easier explaining to children what one hundredweight was than it would be to keep lifting it. The more I thought about it, the more the idea appealed, and I felt very grateful to Deanna. I wanted to express this gratitude in a tangible way, but my brother came back.

After several phone calls, I found the right person to speak to and was told that while applications for teachers' college entry had closed weeks ago, the quota had not been filled. If I attended an interview with a senior school inspector, and he found me to be 'suitable material', it might be possible for me to enrol.

I met the inspector a few days later in a small office at the Auckland Education Board, an organisation that would go the same way as the Astor Hotel, and for much the same reason — cutting corners. He was a dusty-looking man, wearing what seemed like yesterday's shirt and a very narrow tie. His expression suggested that he, too, had thought he was destined for bigger things. He asked for my university results card. He studied it closely, looked at me and looked at the card again.

'But,' he said. 'But you passed. We don't get people who pass.'

I was accepted, and my accidental teaching career was about to start.

2.

ON DAY ONE at Auckland Teachers' College I was told off for not wearing a tie. The same telling-off recurred on many subsequent days, especially Fridays. They were polite and reasonable, quite different from the tellings-off from gown-clad, cane-waving King's College masters, or from the roading foreman when I tipped a load of metal in a pile instead of spreading it nicely along his new road.

'Bring ya bloody shovel next time, ya bloody dopey student bastard,' he yelled, his face reddened by anger and years of outside work.

'Sorry, mate, I didn't know what to do.'

'Don't fuckin' mate me!' he yelled.

I resisted pointing out the possible ambiguity of his statement. I did have a shovel, but I didn't mention this either.

I asked the guys in the pub at the end of the day for advice on spreading metal on roads. An animated discussion followed, with descriptions, diagrams drawn on the back of pay sheets, laughter, and debate about some of the finer points of speed and chain settings, complete with hand gestures and engine noises. It was the sort of discussion that would have made Professor Piddington become even more lavish with his cigarettes and peppermints. The foreman would have been a bit happier too.

Now, as I looked around the room we had been allocated at Auckland Teachers' College, the realisation that I would spend the next two years of my life in this place sank in. It was not a happy feeling. The building seemed old and closed-in; the room didn't feel like a lecture room – with its desks and chairs in neat rows, it felt like a classroom. The windows were high, designed for ventilation, not viewing. I looked around at my fellow students and concluded that they were bereft of brain and beauty. I hadn't seen any of them at university. None of them looked as if they could drive an S-type Bedford.

A middle-aged man walked in and stood at the front. His suit looked as if it had been worn too often, and his tie might well have belonged to his father. He frowned and cleared his throat. It is a tribute, of sorts, to our secondary school training that the throat-clearing noise was sufficient to silence the few conversations in the room. He then proceeded to call the roll, after which he made quite a stirring speech about how important it was, as a teacher, to wear a tie. We were entering a profession, and the symbols of our professionalism, namely ties and shiny shoes, were vital if we were to maintain a necessary distance between ourselves and those we were chosen to lead. How could parents look up to us if we were dressed like truck drivers and kitchen hands? He then asked me and another tieless wretch to meet him in the corridor. I thought I was going to get caned, but received a smaller version of the previous lecture, delivered on the assumption that I hadn't heard it the first time. He then produced two more of his father's ties from the depths of his suit pocket and asked us to wear them. I teetered on refusal but acquiesced – I was on my way to becoming a teacher.

I spent the rest of the week in a cloud of arrogant judgement and general unwillingness. Being here was a mistake, and I needed to either extricate myself or find a way to survive the experience with minimal attendance and involvement. Eventually I began to wear a tie every day, but expressed my independence by choice of colour and clumsy knot-making. It was never an item I wore with ease and I am proud to say that much of my best teaching was done tieless and in scruffy shoes – petty victories, but victories nonetheless.

Of course, things changed. I found that our group, known as a 'section', had the special designation of 'the university section'. We had privileges and totally undeserved status. Paramount among the privileges was time to escape to university. It seemed that the teachers' college would do its absolute best to facilitate our attendance at university lectures during the day, and I ended up with a timetable that would give me most afternoons off. I was taking two units, Stage I Education and Stage II Anthropology. It worried me deeply to find my interest in anthropology was very much higher than in the subject of my chosen, sort of, career.

I started to get to know people. There were initially shy conversations – which school did you go to? Do you think

Peter Snell will break more world records? I didn't really answer the first question but talked enthusiastically about the second. Slowly, the section formed into a series of small groups: the church-goers, the ones who had come straight from school and saw being here as exciting, the misfits, and my group — snobbish pseudo-intellectuals who had spent time at university, usually without success but able to throw names like Camus and Sartre into conversations. We spoke of why the Liszt Piano Concerto was inferior to the Rachmaninoff Number Two, why Bach needed to be revered above all, and why Keith Holyoake was an agricultural clod unfit to run a farm let alone a country. I loved these conversations and thanked Mr L C M Saunders for giving me so much ammunition. We would sit with our group in the cafeteria, cigarettes in our hands, and talk loudly as we drank our instant coffee and ate our sausage rolls. In recollection, much of this conversation makes me blush, especially when I think of how willing we were to air our views in the hearing of others.

We treated lecturers with disdain, as one must. Some of this was justified in that they were primary school teachers who tried to run their lectures as if they were in their primary school classrooms. They did not encourage discussion and failed to see that their prepared notes did not, as yet, have any relevance for us. We didn't know what we were looking for, but did know this wasn't it.

AFTER ABOUT FOUR WEEKS, everything changed. We were taken, en masse, to observe a classroom at Normal

Intermediate School. I have never understood the rationale for calling this school 'Normal'. It was associated with the teachers' college and had a significant role in our training. It was supposed to offer a high standard of education, and parents competed to have their children enrolled there, but it had a tense, pressure-cooker atmosphere which I hoped was far from normal. The name persists today, which suggests that there are many people for whom success means being called 'normal'.

We shuffled into the school, suddenly wary of doing the wrong thing. I was conscious of not having been into a primary school for many years, and never having entered that strange educational compromise called intermediate school. The creation of intermediate schools was to be one of my first sources of educational outrage, but more of that later. We were broken up into groups of five or six and told to move as unobtrusively as we could to the back of our appointed classroom. Somehow, I ended up at the side of the classroom, which gave me the enormous advantage of being able to see the children's faces. They were well accustomed to being guinea pigs and took little notice of us, a gauche group of potential teachers, women all in dresses, men with an assortment of strange ties.

The teacher, tieless, sleeves rolled up, was energetically explaining the mysteries of long division. The class clearly liked him, his bouncy style and his little jokes, but they seemed to have no idea of what he was talking about. I was spellbound, watching the faces, some showing understanding, most reflecting various reactions to being lost. Why, I wondered, were we supposed to be standing at the back, where children's comprehension, or lack of it, would be seen only in extreme cases? Why didn't the teacher see what I saw and stop? But he didn't. It was easy to think he had picked out the faces that had the glow of understanding and was talking to them. Why didn't he break them up into groups, one for those who could see that the 27 bags of coins he was talking about could only be taken a certain number of times from the stockpile of 468, and several other groups, some of whom would have had trouble if the bags could take three coins and the stockpile was only nine? Why didn't he have piles of coins for them to count out, to see, to hold?

He asked for a volunteer to come up to the blackboard and demonstrate how they would approach 948 divided by 36. I sensed I was not alone in hoping not to be picked out for this. Several hands went up, and he selected a pupil whose uniform seemed more crisply ironed than everyone else's. She powered through the task, talking quietly as she went, writing on the blackboard in small, neat figures and arriving at 26 with '... three and a bit more left over'. She smiled at the teacher, he smiled at her and then smiled at us, a quiet smile of triumph that, to me, said, 'See, I have successfully taught this quite complex mathematical procedure.' He showered the girl with praise, which she accepted with an aplomb that suggested she was not unaccustomed to being praised. She was given house points and group points, whatever they may have been. She was clearly pleased to get them. One of the boys was looking at me. I winked. He lifted his hands, palms upwards, pushed out his bottom lip and shrugged his shoulders. Clearly, no house points or group points for him today.

Back at teachers' college we were told about the high quality of the teaching we had seen, how the level of class control and organisation were things we would have to work on for years to achieve.

'But they didn't understand. Half of them, more than half, didn't understand!' I told the lecturer, smoke coming out of my indignant nostrils.

I wanted to swear. I wanted to be as direct and angry as the roading foreman, but I wasn't.

'Well,' said our lecturer, 'sometimes you have to go over a topic several times before everyone gets it. What you saw was a model lesson conducted in a model classroom. And weren't you asked to stand at the back of the room? You may well have distracted many of the pupils.'

I said 'Crap', very quietly indeed. I wanted to say you couldn't expect thirty-five children to understand a lesson delivered as if they were all at the same level. I wanted to say I saw children being harmed because they had reached the conclusion that division was something they would never be able to do.

I felt, for the first time since I'd entered the doors of this place, a fire in my belly. That fire was to last for the rest of my teaching career. Perhaps it is not too much to say for the rest of my life. I know I feel it stirring as I write about this first classroom experience. At times the fire has burned bright, almost out of control. It has often been just a smouldering ember when other crises, real and imagined, robbed me of energy for teaching. And there have been times when I have felt that educational hierarchies have aimed the extinguishers of convention at it, dampening things but not quite putting them out.

From then on I think I became an arrogant pain in the arse, constantly challenging, often with the backing of ideas and facts that needed more research. I read books like Herbert Read's *Education Through Art*, fascinated but also looking for quotable quotes. Many of my statements should have been questions and many of my questions were really statements. I became a crusader for the abolition of intermediate schools. The first intermediate school in New Zealand was Kōwhai Intermediate in the Auckland suburb of Sandringham, established in 1922. It is about half a mile (we are still in Imperial-almost-everything days) from that glorious temple of New Zealand sporting ambition and history – Eden Park.

Before its establishment, many scholars and administrators toyed with the idea of a three-level education system. The first would be primary school, where children would stay for six years. This would be followed by four years in a junior high school. In these two levels students would be given a general education, although in the fourth year at junior high some students, who had been identified as having reached their potential, would be given a 'finishing' programme designed to be of practical help in the big wide world they were about to join. After junior high there would be a series of specialised high schools, where students would be able to pursue the strengths they had shown thus far. Some high schools would be academic, which probably meant everyone had to learn Latin. Others would focus on the sciences, or technology or music – I'm not sure about music, but I like the idea of students being able to focus on their musical talents for three years. Mind you, I also wanted students, in all schools, to have the Mr L C M Saunders musical experience. I can just hear my teachers' college lecturer say, 'You can't have it both ways. Interesting ideas but more thought needed!'

Even now I still see the benefits of this structure, benefits that can't really be fully developed in a two-year intermediate school. Those who favour intermediate schools, and some of my best friends do, speak of the value of having large groups of students the same age all together. This is true for many students – the bright girl who displayed her ability to master the complexities of long division would probably thrive. Many others are, I believe, disturbed by the shortness of their time there and by their rank within the system. Almost all the early intermediates had graded classes. A test was given at the start of the year and this would determine placement for the following two years. The most popular of these tests had been developed in France or the United States. They purported to measure intelligence but, inevitably, they measured other things, like participation in mainstream culture and the socio-economic status of parents. At the time Dr Pat Hohepa developed an 'IQ Test for Tangata Whenua' which included questions like 'How do you cook puha?' and 'What is a hinaki?' Some people got the point.

Whatever grading method was used, children, unlike eggs or fruit or stones for the road, knew where they stood. You could be blatant and call the classes A to H, or something obscure, like the names of New Zealand's Governors-General, but everyone knew who was top and who was bottom and acted accordingly.

In my view, then and now, the junior high school debate was not given full airing and was scuttled by that most powerful of determiners of educational structure and ambition: economics. Intermediate schools were the cheapest and quickest way to solve the problem of rising school rolls. Kōwhai Intermediate remains an excellent school, one I sent two of my children to, but I do wish there had been a Kōwhai Junior High School for them to go to.

TOWARDS THE END of Term One our section was sent on 'section'. The word, at teachers' college, meant both a group and an action. The vagaries of the English language have ascribed a variety of other meanings, ranging from a plot of land to the process of being admitted to a mental institution. In this case it meant being assigned to a classroom for a period of four weeks to learn from the associate teacher, the less-than-grandiose title given to the classroom teacher. We were all excited, and a little apprehensive, about going on section. Tales from second-year students circulated, some of them of sections where the associate went to the staffroom to smoke cigarettes and drink coffee while the hapless student tried to run the class; some about being sat in the corner, an anonymous figure ignored by teacher and students alike.

Most of us were sent back to Normal Intermediate — clearly, we were better to start with normal and work our way outwards from there. My associate was, I thought, middle-aged, which at the time equated to being over thirty. She was efficient and businesslike, with worksheets for the kids and worksheets for me. I was to observe, write descriptions of lessons, pick two or three students and record what I saw as their needs. It was not expected that I would be ready to take a lesson.

She hadn't counted on the fire that had been ignited on my first visit to her school. I was restless in my desire to stand in front of the class and teach. (My concept of teaching was still limited to the idea that a teacher stood at the front and dispensed learning to the waiting students, whose receptiveness depended largely on the quality of the performance.) I completed the assigned tasks in the first week, learned everyone's names, helped the individuals I thought needed it and joined in their lunchtime games. The associate was impressed. Amused, perhaps, by my naïve enthusiasm, but impressed enough to say that, despite what was normally done, I could conduct the next day's spelling test. My first lesson! I took the list of words home, made sure I could spell them, and wrote a detailed lesson plan, using pens of several colours.

I felt as nervous as I had at boxing tournaments but, when the time came, climbed into the ring and went for it. Thirty faces of thirty well-trained twelve-year-olds gazed at me. They were accustomed to students and knew they had the power to make or break, knew that my stumbling first attempts would require their patience, understanding and, if need be, their mockery. I had that sense of elation that comes from being on stage, and began the lesson with a flourish.

'Apple – Jimmy brought an apple to school but William stole it. Apple.'

Jimmy and William looked up, startled but amused.

I managed to weave all their names into the test. There

was laughter, protest and a sense of expectation from those yet to be named. It had nothing to do with my lesson plan; it was fun, wholehearted, show-off fun, the best spelling test I ever conducted. I knew I was modelling myself on Mr L C M Saunders, albeit with spelling words rather than the grandeur of opera.

My associate was uncertain about whether she should approve, but found herself smiling and then showered me with praise. We planned further teaching I could do, including the special lesson to be delivered in front of my lecturer. Of all her words, the ones that I remembered in detail were: 'That lesson was brilliant and brilliance, every now and then, is a great thing. But teaching requires more than brilliance – it requires preparation and stamina.' Three years later, when I was in my own classroom, the meaning of her second sentence, which I had largely ignored, came back to haunt me. I realised that although I had bounced on the trampoline, it was the associate who had set it up and made it possible for ambitious show-offs like me to bounce high.

SECTIONS WERE TO BECOME the highlights of my time at teachers' college, and the one at now-defunct Napier Street School was to have the most influence. In the early 1960s there was an influx of people from the Pacific Islands to New Zealand. The majority of those who settled in Auckland went to Ponsonby or Grey Lynn, where, to quote a neighbour who raced around town installing people's first TVs, 'If need be, you can buy an old dunger of a villa, a villa in Grey Lynn or

Ponsonby, for a few hundred pounds.' It was another twenty years before I took up this advice.

The children of these Pasifika families went to Napier Street or neighbouring Beresford Street schools. At teachers' college there was much speculation about how difficult they might be to work in. Students who had been to one of them had a certain status, and their opinions were sought by those of us who found we were scheduled to follow them. And dammit, these opinions, informed by the benign unconscious racism of my middle-class colleagues, ignited another fire. Some labelled the Pasifika pupils as needing a very firm hand, and explained how, to succeed as a student, you needed to be tough, far tougher than you would be in other circumstances. Others spoke of how charming the children were with their big brown eyes, their desire to touch you and their beautiful singing. This admiration was accompanied by a sense of reduced expectations — they were lovely, but they weren't going to learn much. I was going to battle against this attitude many times in the future.

Pasifika parents were here because they wanted their children to obtain an education. Some of their expectations were unrealistic, even damaging, but they knew that without education, it would not have been worth the upheaval of coming to New Zealand. I thought of the truck drivers who had spoken of their distress at having to leave home in the dark and for it to be dark again when they got home. 'It's for my kids and for the education.' This was a sentence I heard repeated time and again, both in the Astor Hotel and in many schools in the years to come.

Teachers' college was highlighted by the occasional inspiring lecture and by the opportunities to become involved in my university studies. In my second year my university courses were Anthropology II and Maori Studies I. I was lucky enough to be taught by vibrant, politically active lecturers – Bruce Biggs (responsible for my enduring affection for the double vowel in te reo, irrespective of the current preference for macrons), Pat Hohepa, Robert Mahuta, Hirini Mead, Pita Sharples, Hugh Kawharu and Tony Hooper come to mind. Classes were small and took place, mainly, in old villas in Symonds Street. Somehow, being away from a lecture hall made the sessions feel more like discussion and debate than formal lectures. I found it quite easy to keep up with the work, partly because there were few other demands on my time, but mainly because my interest was captured. I felt not just fully involved in my studies but excited by them. I also collected lots of ammunition to throw around back at college – ammunition I used both wisely and unwisely.

In my second year, Ranginui Walker joined the teachers' college staff. For the first time there was a lecturer with ammunition to fire at me, to fire at all of us. His life is well summarised in Tom Fitzsimons' obituary in the *Dominion* of 3 March 2016.

Ranginui Walker was one of New Zealand's most recognisable and forceful advocates for Maori.

He was an academic, but hardly a cloistered one. With regular magazine columns and television appearances, university courses popular among Maori and Pakeha alike, and significant books written for a general readership, he took his essential argument – that Maori had been severely and enduringly wronged by colonisation – directly to the public.

His work was part of a wave of commentary and activism from the 1970s and 1980s that shattered the broad Pakeha consensus that New Zealand's race relations were ideal.

Suddenly, teachers' college, on certain days, became exciting. Ranginui was just starting to emerge as a commentator, and was viewed by mainstream New Zealand as a radical, an ungrateful troublemaker fiddling with a Pandora's Box of grievances that were better left alone, better ignored, as they had been for the past 150 years.

I was playing rugby at the time, for the Teachers College Club, second grade. The club was on a roll, with the premier team, bolstered by players like Jim Maniapoto who later played with the New Zealand Māori, doing better than ever before in the cut-throat Auckland competition. Jim was in our section. He was large, smiling and quiet. On his first game with the Auckland provincial team, the commentator described him as 'half as big again as a Māori meeting house'. We decided, over our coffee cups, that while this might have been apt, it was not acceptable.

Our team, meantime, was a bit of a hotchpotch, with a coach who wanted to be somewhere else, a high turnover of players, and none of the 'death is better than defeat' spirit of school days. We lurched along, and then Ranginui, out of either sympathy or a desire for exercise, persuaded himself and his thirty-plus body to join us. It was a great boost. In one particular game, the Auckland selector for the grade was on the sideline. One of the opposition took advantage of a deep dark ruck and whacked Ranginui on the nose. His nose was, to put it politely, quite prominent, as was the pain from the whack. For the next few minutes he played like a man possessed, tackling, running and chanting. His efforts caught the selector's eye. He stopped play and asked, 'What's the name of the Māori boy?'

Ranginui, already fired up, was incensed.

'Did you say Māori boy?' he demanded.

'Yeah, Māori boy, you, what's your name?'

Ranginui then delivered quite a long speech about how retaining and using diminutive words like 'boy' for fully grown adults was an example of the colonial attitudes that were preventing race relations in this country from making any progress. Some of us went and stood beside him, others wondered what it was all about.

'Okay,' said the selector. 'I see you don't want to be in the rep team!'

With that, he wandered back to his car and drove off, probably to Eden Park, where he could meet up with beer-drinking administrative mates to whom he would relate the story as an amusing example of how stroppy 'them bloody Maoris' were starting to become. They would laugh and then become serious as they thought of the possible threats to upcoming tours to and from South Africa. None of us realised how momentous 1981 was going to be.

IN MY FIRST FEW DAYS at teachers' college I had done my usual defensive trick of deciding everyone was inferior and not worthy of my attention. It did take a bit of time, but I slowly discovered that in my section there were intelligent and beautiful people after all. By intelligent I suppose I mean they shared some of my ideas; by beautiful I mean they agreed to go out with me. It has taken me a lifetime to appreciate the constant surprise that people can be once they haven't had the fetters of my own limitations imposed on them.

I think the first friend I made was Peter. He was a tall, well-built man, a year or two older than me. He was married and had two children, which filled me with awe. I was twenty years old and had never had a married friend. In addition, Peter drove trucks in the holidays for a firm called Pengelly's. This firm was famous for its fleet of older trucks, early-model Bedfords with genuine 'crash gearboxes'. If you didn't time the gear change to match it accurately with the engine revs, everyone in earshot would know that you had missed a change. In addition, a faulty change could jar your wrist and result in serious loss of power as the old bones of the truck laboured uphill. Peter reckoned that after three summers with the firm, he could just about get it right every time. He had, every now and then, driven trucks with big trailers, a level of achievement I never reached. Truck-and-trailer drivers were the postgraduates of the trade, usually older drivers able to back accurately and undertake long-haul journeys. As well as being acknowledged for their skill, these drivers usually had their trucks loaded and unloaded by machines — no more of the asbestos and cement we lesser beings had to heave around.

Peter and I developed a lifelong friendship forged by involvement in each other's disasters and a remarkable amount of furniture moving. My children call him 'Uncle Peter', his children call me 'Uncle Tim'. This honorary avuncular status fills me with smiles.

Ken arrived in our section about a month after the year had started. He was from New York, and in New Zealand because of his opposition to American nuclear policy. He wore thick black-framed glasses and immediately seemed clever and thoughtful. Soon after he arrived, the section went on a visit to Beresford Street School in Howe Street, in the suburb of Freemans Bay. Our observations finished at midday and we were free to wander off to university. Ken, to whom I'd said little more than a friendly hello, asked if he could walk with Peter and me. On the way there we passed the Civic Hotel at the bottom of Wellesley Street. Well, we didn't actually pass. We debated the heat of the day, the need to talk about the school visit, the fact that lectures didn't start for a while, and made our way down the stairs to the welcoming gloom of the bar with its carpet of turquoise swirls and paintings from the brewery-sponsored Kelliher Art Competition on the walls, a competition that seemed to favour heavy bush scenes and a palate of brown and green.

After the second beer I explained to Ken what was wrong with American foreign policy — there was a lot wrong, so it took quite a while. He listened in attentive silence and, when I had finally run out, said, 'You are totally right. You're also a complete bastard for dumping it all on me before this terrible New Zealand beer has had time to numb me a bit.'

This is how long and enduring friendships begin.

3.

MY SECOND YEAR at teachers' college, 1963, was a comfortable romp, highlighted by times on section, the demands of university and blossoming friendships. One of these friendships was with Eseta, a sparkling young woman from Tonga who had joined our section halfway through the previous year. I adored her full response to life – she would laugh and the whole room would laugh. More than that, if she was sad, she cried great gushing uninhibited tears. The tears I had witnessed when I was growing up never involved anything more than small sniffs and ironed handkerchiefs. Eseta's enthusiastic bursts of sadness seemed like a miracle. She was clever and funny and had a burning desire to become a teacher.

On one section, she was listening to a Tongan boy read. He stumbled on the word 'octopus' and she gave him the Tongan translation, *feke*. Several other kids heard, and they started discussing their words for octopus – it is one of many words that appear, in slightly different forms, in most Pacific languages. Māori say wheke, Sāmoans *fe'e*. The discussion broadened into finding other words that were similar in their various home languages. The discussion was interrupted by Eseta's associate, and she was subsequently counselled by the principal and various people from teachers' college. Everyone knew she was trying to help, but she needed to realise that she was seriously disadvantaging the children.

The word feke came to symbolise what some of us were wanting to achieve in the education of the many Pacific Island children entering the country. We resolved that when we had our own classrooms, we would have a large picture of an octopus on the wall to symbolise our openness to other languages.

One weekend, Eseta and I were walking on the rocks at the northern end of Ōrewa Beach — we did things like that, despite her strict Methodist beliefs and the fact that she lived at 'Atalanga, the Tongan Queen's Epsom residence. On this occasion we encountered a small octopus in a rock pool. She grabbed it, and its tentacles grabbed her arm. She stripped them away, turned it upside down, pressed it against her mouth and bit something. The octopus ceased struggling and hung from her hand like a piece of seaweed, dripping dark nautical ooze. I was truly, madly, deeply impressed. I don't know if you have ever kissed someone who has just bitten an octopus. It is a very special experience, but not an easy one to organise.

J K Hunn's 'Report on [the] Department of Maori Affairs' was not so much published as quietly released in 1961. In it, Māori urbanisation was discussed, and a variety of problems outlined. Hunn saw the solution in the assimilation of Māori into Pākehā culture through intermarriage and education.

He regarded the retention of Māori language and culture as impediments to development and likely causes of 'colour problems'. There would be no feke in his classroom.

We were galvanised by this, but we were not a large 'we'. I saw so many of my fellow students, tomorrow's teachers, good, caring people, content to accept Hunn's wisdom and do their best to help brown children be part of mainstream society, to become assimilated. 'Assimilation,' as I remember Dr Pat Hohepa saying in a lecture, 'is what the shark said to the snapper.'

There were other fights to be fought: nuclear testing was becoming more of a worry, especially with the French eyeing up the Pacific as a safe testing area — safe, that is, for people living in France. We had been through the Cuban missile crisis and believed nuclear war could, by either accident or design, happen at any minute. I knew I had to protest, do whatever small thing waving a banner could do.

In my first year at university, I had heard that a protest march was organised for a Thursday lunchtime. I had a lecture that day from eleven to twelve, but I sat near the door so I could slip out early. I knew there would be a crowd, and didn't want to be late and miss out on one of the banners provided by the organisers. When I got to our rallying point, the band rotunda in Albert Park, I thought I had the wrong day. There were twelve people there, thirteen with me. Thirteen, to march down Queen Street, protesting about a policy the majority of citizens either didn't know about or supported. I had heard people, some in my own family, some in my section, say that the development of nuclear weapons, of the American nuclear umbrella, was the only way we would be saved from communism, from the Asian hordes that wanted our green paddocks and the dissolution of the Empire.

A barber who had noted my anti-nuclear badge had told me: 'Ya know, if all those bloody South East Asians bring themselves down here, you'll never get another roast dinner. The buggers'll eat all our bloody sheep, you just watch them. Then they'll start on the bloody fish!' Protest was also seen as offensive to the RSA and the heroes of World War Two and the Korean War. One of my father's friends, a veteran of both conflicts, his fists shaking and his jaw jutting, told me not to insult the memory of his fallen comrades.

Protest, I realised, would probably be futile, but I had to pick up my banner and trudge reluctantly off as one of the thirteen. The police sergeant assigned, with two constables, to guide and protect us, clearly thought he had drawn the short straw that day. He instructed us not to walk on the road, as planned. 'You're such a pathetic group, the footpath will do. Walk swiftly, watch out for prams and get it over and done with as quick as possible. And if any of you buggers try sitting down to stop the traffic, just know, we will pull yous up by the ears, ya bloody ears, got it?'

My vision of surging down Queen Street, part of a triumphant, chanting multitude, was changed to a shuffling little group of leftovers, heads down, banners high. Needless to say, I saw just about everyone I knew. Friends of my parents on their way to shop at Smith & Caughey's either looked at me or looked away. One asked the standard older-person question: 'How are things going at school? Is this some kind of school project?' I saw several guys I had been to school with. They had swapped the uniform of school for the uniform of business: grey suit, white shirt and old boys' tie. One yelled, 'Bloody hell, Heath, haven't you grown out of being a bloody commie yet?' I had liked him, played in the same rugby team for a few years, and once been invited to his lavish birthday party in an exceptionally large house in the eastern suburbs. His words made me feel unexpectedly sad, not because of their content or the fact that he chose to publicly yell at me. It was more because of the realisation that there were paths to be chosen and that mine would take me away from many comfortable things of the past. I gave him the fingers and raised my banner a bit higher.

A truck stopped beside us. The driver leaned out. He recognised me. He laughed, he waved, he made gestures involving grimaces and waving his fingers above his head. As he drove off, he waved with a clownish vigour that suggested he had hatched a plan. He drove back and performed the old trick of turning off the ignition for a few seconds, letting the truck coast, and then turning on the key again, making the engine deliver an ear-shattering backfire. He kept doing this until the police sergeant's amusement started to wear thin.

It was a long way back to the university.

MUCH TO MY DELIGHT, I went on section to Beresford Street, the school I had loved visiting the previous year. It was packed with children from the Pacific, children I knew I wanted to teach. My associate, Dave, was an old-fashioned teacher whose saving graces were his sense of humour and his extraordinary love of rugby. He had once been hooker in the Auckland team and was pleased that I knew this. I don't think I modelled much of my teaching on him, apart from the fact that we had fun and went to the pub as often as possible. One morning, he and the teacher in the next classroom had an argument that somehow escalated into fisticuffs. Just when this started to become more serious, and I, the wide-eyed student, didn't know whether to run or hide, the headmaster came in.

'Stop!' he bellowed.

'My office in five minutes, clean and tidy!' he bellowed.

Two sheepish forty-year-old men duly turned up at his office. He made them stand in front of his desk for a considerable time, silent and unsmiling, before reaching into the drawer, taking out two lollies and giving them one each.

WHERE WAS I back in 1963 when John F Kennedy was assassinated? I was at my parents' house, in the laundry, doing my week's washing. My father called me to the phone.

'They've shot him,' Eseta said.

I knew who she meant. She came over. Other friends came over. These were the wonderful days of 'coming over' and of using the telephone to arrange where to meet. On this occasion it was Albert Park, by one of the fantastical Morton Bay fig trees. We wandered about the park, sad, shocked, worried.

Kennedy had our approval, though not fully. Catholicism, birth control, the Bay of Pigs, Marilyn Monroe – he had a lot to answer for in the Court of Undergraduate Wisdom. But he was the first American President, the first world leader, we could identify with. We felt a closeness with his age, his activities and his aspirations. His death took some hope away, some feeling of involvement, and we wept. Wept more than we should, hindsight would suggest, but weep we did for him, his family and the political doors we saw slamming shut. Martin Luther King was gaining our ears, the troubles in Vietnam were escalating, our first full-time year of teaching was looming, and The Beatles were starting to fill our heads and move our feet – so much happened in 1963.

I was granted the full-time final year at university, just as the lovely Deanna Tamborini had promised. I would be on the same pay my friends and colleagues received for working their hearts out in their classrooms. A part of me envied them those classrooms, and I couldn't wait until I had my own, but a much larger part knew how lucky I was to be in a time when the teaching profession so desperately longed for the respectability it believed university graduation would bring.

I had to teach in the weeks when university was not operating, and ended up at a suburban school, taking the class of a tired deputy principal so he could be freed for 'administration'. He was delighted to be released from the need to crank himself up for yet another year. I hurled myself into the task, and the kids and I had something that had been missing from their classroom life – fun. We enjoyed summer, stories and games outside; we spread paint far and wide. We enjoyed the energy I was able to expend, knowing I would be released at the beginning of March.

The deputy principal was a good man who ran a well-organised, prosaic classroom in which learning happened. He was neither unkind nor inspiring. In hindsight, I think I did him a disservice. He taught me one great lesson, one that came back to haunt me — as soon as you are tired of teaching, you have to stop. I don't mean the day-to-day weariness that comes after spending six hours with the energy of children, or even the end-of-term fatigue when you have been up too late at night writing reports. I mean the emptiness that comes when you realise that you can't do it any more, that you truly don't want to do it any more. The spark and the reward have been replaced with boredom, a desire to be punitive and an overwhelming urge to go to sleep at two in the afternoon. We, fresh-faced students that we were, all vowed to tell each other if we saw this happening. We never did.

Study in 1964 was a joy. I wasn't taking Education, which was a relief. Social Anthropology was a challenge but a rewarding one, and I decided I wanted to go on to do an MA in Anthropology, though wasn't sure when I would fit it in. There was so much I wanted to do. I listened to friends talking about their OE plans, which shipping line was the cheapest, whether it was best to stay in London or a smaller city, and a host of other questions. I was surprised, and grateful, to realise that while the fascination of going overseas, of seeing the place my New Zealand-born father called 'home', was huge, my real dream was to stand in front of my own classroom.

At the end of 1964, Eseta went back to Tonga. We farewelled each other on the wharf before she boarded the Union Steamship Company's *Matua* for the crowded and

stuffy journey home. Our farewell was tearful and difficult —
we both knew we would not see each other again. Her need
to work in schools in Tonga was overwhelming and I wasn't
ready to go there. The ship sailed, we wrote each other long
letters for a while, and then left it at that. I had, still have, a lot
of smiley memories, some of them tinged with sea creatures. I
also had an unexpected sense of relief at no longer having to
negotiate the rules and quirks of another culture — so much
more difficult in practice than in reading an anthropological
text. I would, henceforth, stay firmly in my own paddock.

I was now a graduate, with a BA and a Teaching Diploma.
I was scheduled to start teaching at Huapai Primary School,
some thirty kilometres north of Auckland. I hadn't heard of
Huapai and wasn't sure whether I wanted to go there, but it
had the advantage of being a one-year appointment rather
than the usual two years. The New Zealand birth rate in the early
1960s was the highest it had ever been, and these were times of
teacher shortage. This meant people like me could apply for a
position of whatever duration we wanted. My thought was to
spend a year learning, making my mistakes, and then to move
on to a fresh start, armed, forewarned and on top.

It was a good theory.

4.

SOMETIMES WHEN YOU meet people for the first time
the process is protracted in a way that makes you feel you know
quite a lot about them before the first handshake. That is how
it was when I met Wes, the deputy principal at Huapai School. I
had ridden my motorbike up the rough metal driveway behind
the school on the first day of Term One 1965. I would like to say
I 'roared' up the driveway, but it was a small bike and it didn't
roar. I stopped, in a slightly sideways manner, heaved myself
back to balance, and proceeded to fumble with my helmet
and gloves. Wes had also just arrived. He came over to me and
stood, with smile and outstretched hand, waiting for me to get
myself organised. By the time we shook hands, we were both
laughing – as we did throughout a friendship that lasted until
his untimely death in 2002.

I had contacted the headmaster shortly after Christmas. He
was not impressed by my enthusiasm and told me to come
back at the beginning of the term. I had also strolled around
the school in the weekend, noting its extensive grounds and

mixture of old and new buildings. I hoped my classroom would be in an old building. Then, and now, I saw classrooms as workspaces, not shop fronts. A pristine classroom is a sad place. I had visions of covering the walls with artwork and having paint, glue and crayons permanently at the ready. I had read the great creative education advocates of the time: the aforementioned Herbert Read's *Education Through Art*; Elwyn Richardson's *In the Early World*; Sylvia Ashton-Warner. They were my heroes, all the more so because the last two were New Zealanders. Notions of releasing creativity raced around my head – I was going to need an old classroom.

That morning I attended my first staff meeting. I was the only one sitting on the edge of my chair, focusing on every word, taking notes, smiling at anyone who looked at me. Well, I did for the first thirty minutes. There was a lot of talk about routines, behaviour at assemblies, washing staffroom teacups and the distribution of milk. It was like being on a much-anticipated date but then finding we had nothing in common. But then I was given my class list. I pored over it – the thirty-two names of the Standard Three and Four girls and boys who were being entrusted to me for the year. Names that meant nothing but would come to mean everything. Strangely, as I write this some fifty-five years later, I can remember most of the names, see most of the faces.

'Now,' said Alan the headmaster. 'You, young Tim, will be having Room Six. Some teachers think it's a bit shabby, but who knows, you might quite enjoy its . . . what shall we say, its freedom.' He looked around the room, exchanging knowing smiles with a few teachers. 'Yes,' he continued, 'Room Six. I am sure you will be able to brighten it up a bit, make it nicer than the draughty old barn it has been labelled by some of your colleagues.'

I was the new chum, getting the worst of it. Getting the truck with the clunky gearbox and the windows that wouldn't wind up. I grinned happily at the prospect of a draughty old barn. I think the headmaster saw me as a bit simple but admirably compliant.

The room was a delight — big, with benches around the walls, and tall double-hung windows. I could see treetops, which seemed important. The floor was made of well-trodden wooden planks. Grainy dirt was packed into the gaps between the boards. I climbed on a desk and jumped, landing as hard as I could on the floor. Dirt erupted from the gaps and cracks, then fell back to form little mountain ranges along the planks. I laughed — this was going to be a happy date.

I couldn't wait for the children to arrive the next day. I was there early, unlocked my own classroom and fussed around. I was dressed for the part — crimplene shorts, well-ironed cotton shirt, tie (of course), and grey socks pulled up to the knee. Wes came in to wish me well for the day, and I suddenly realised I was nervous. His lack of a tie was instantly influential.

'Show them who's boss, mate, then you can ease up and be friends later. If they think you're too nice, they'll walk all over you.'

I had heard this advice before but didn't think it applied to me. In my class we were all going to bond instantly and wander off joyously along a trail of learning, laughter and mutual respect.

Bells rang, names were read out, lines were formed, instructions were bellowed and then, magically, there was a series of straight lines, barefooted kids trying to stand still on February's hot asphalt.

'Room Six,' instructed the headmaster, 'turn left and follow Mr Heath to your classroom.'

I waved my hand in the air, like a cowboy with a lasso. I'm not sure why, but they took it as a signal to move forward. We arrived at Room Six. I opened the door and indicated that they should go in. In my rehearsal of this, the children would move slowly while I chatted with each of them, warm and reassuring. The reality was they rushed in, fought over desks and kicked up a hell of a racket.

I yelled my first words to my precious first class. 'This is not good enough!'

Then I made them line up again and come in silently.

Wes came past, grinning. 'Can't you fellas find the door?' he asked. Half the class laughed — I didn't.

We spent the day sitting in silence, children writing meaningless nonsense and me prowling like a sergeant major.

'Good man,' said the headmaster when I flopped into the staffroom for a cup of tea at the end of the day. 'You are really establishing yourself with them. I could hear you all the way to my office.'

Wes walked in and saluted me.

I went home and drafted my letter of resignation.

The next day I resolved to be something resembling a reasonable human being. I would be kind and entertaining. If the kids climbed the walls, so be it.

The bell rang, they lined up perfectly, marched in quietly, sat down silently and waited for me to call the roll. Except I couldn't, because I kept laughing and making silly jokes about their names. I think, at that moment, the kids realised that if there was going to be any order in the place, they would have to keep it.

'Who would like to go outside and run from here to the gate and all around the field before we do our arithmetic?' I asked.

They all would, so we went for a romp in the sunshine, me bringing up the rear, encouraging the stragglers. We laughed and puffed and were reluctant to go back inside for the joys of mental arithmetic.

At morning tea, one of the older teachers said, 'Looks like you're having a bit of a problem keeping your lot from running away. Saw you had to chase them. Got some real bad eggs in there, I reckon. Got to keep on top of 'em, keep 'em inside at least.'

I grinned — he didn't.

After that, we went for a run every morning if it wasn't raining — and often when it was, since this seemed to make them even happier. They had forgiven me for being a jerk on day one and we started to have fun. But I came to realise that while the morning run was great, it wasn't enough. Classrooms are unnatural places for young growing children to be. Kids are not programmed for sitting still. We fell into a pattern of going outside to run and jump and play at least three times a day. I used it as a bribe: 'Finish your stories by half past eleven and we can go outside until lunchtime.' These were kids from the small farms, orchards and vineyards of Huapai and Kumeu — fields that would one day be subjected to the rigid discipline of growing kiwifruit. These were children who understood physical activity. Of course some excelled and some struggled, but there was, surprisingly perhaps, no one who didn't want to take part.

On our timetable I assigned all of Friday morning for art. Alan called me in for a serious chat.

'I am aware you spend a hell of a lot of time outside,' he said, 'more than the physical education syllabus requires, but I am turning a blind eye to this because the children seem, well, happy. But art in the morning? No, no, no. The morning, when minds are fresh, is for arithmetic and spelling and essay writing. Art is Friday afternoon when everyone is a bit tired and needs to relax.'

I gave him the full Sylvia Ashton-Warner, Elwyn Richardson and Herbert Read speech. I told him Director of Education Clarence Beeby wanted teachers to experiment 'without the burden of having to succeed'. I hoped he hadn't realised Dr Beeby resigned in 1960.

He tapped the ash off his cigarette, cupped his chin in his hand, and looked me up and down.

'Well,' he said, 'I suppose this is what you get from going to university and who am I to argue, even if I have been teaching for forty years, forty bloody years. Do it your way, but if the parents come down on you like a ton of bricks, don't come crying to me!'

They didn't and I didn't.

I thought the children's Friday morning paintings were marvellous. I made impassioned speeches about just being themselves when they painted, that there was no right way, no best and no worst. All that mattered was they let themselves become absorbed in the task, let it become the most important thing in the world.

Wes told me he had been standing outside my room when I made one of these speeches. 'Heck,' he said, 'I thought bloody Winston Churchill was in there.'

He said this as a joke, but it quite pleased me. What pleased me most was that when the children really gave themselves to their painting, or crayon drawings, they no longer seemed to notice if I was there. I tried to emphasise the process of creating a picture and not focus on results. But I thought the results were fabulous and festooned all of Room Six's old walls with them.

Of the many good memories I have of that magical year, one stands out beyond all the others. I was reading a great book: *Another Country* by James Baldwin. I sat under a tree at lunchtime, book in one hand, school pie in the other, totally absorbed, but the damned bell went. Back in the classroom, I knew I had to read some more.

'Look, Class, I just have to keep reading this book. It's so good, so exciting. So what say you get out your books and we will all read, all enjoy our books for the next twenty minutes or so. But, we'll have to be real quiet in case anyone finds out.'

They entered the conspiracy and gave themselves to the series of tatty library books they had, few of them as interesting as James Baldwin. I finished the chapter and was able to focus on being a real teacher again. Except, when I look back, I think I was closer to being a real teacher when we all read together than I was in the lesson that followed: 'Sheep farming in New Zealand'.

There were many special classes over the years, but Room Six at Huapai Primary, in 1965, was extra-special. I would love to meet them again, to see if their memories are as warm as mine, to find out what sort of people they have become.

MY APPOINTMENT AT Huapai was only for one year. Suddenly it was October and I had to think about what to do next. What you did next in New Zealand teaching in the 1960s, and for many painful years after that, was to get a 'top grading'. This complex and humiliating system involved a school inspector visiting for a day and allocating a mark, which was then given to you in a report. Reports were different colours: white, green and yellow. A beginning teacher could only apply for a White Report. White Report grades went up to seven, but you could only get a maximum of four points on each triannual grading. You needed to be older, with sagging enthusiasm and gut, before you could apply for the seemingly unobtainable heights of Green and Yellow.

In addition, there were comments written on the reports, terse abbreviations: G, VG and Ex. The number of comments was significant, in that the grading number was the key to winning jobs – a four with three comments beat a four with two comments in the poker game of appointment. Suitability for a position was not considered. An old lag who had ground out a grading of five over twelve years would be appointed over a young gun who had scored four first up. I don't know why we put up with it, why I was so satisfied many years later to have reached the top of both Green and Yellow, to have become one of those people we spoke of with awe: 'He's/she's a Green Seven and a Yellow Five!'

My 1965 grading meant that I could shop for jobs, including the position of sole teacher in a rural school. I flirted with the idea of doing this, listed all the pros and cons, talked with Wes for hours about it, even talked with Alan. I should have admitted, right at the start, that I was in love with the idea. I saw having my own little school as romantic and exciting. The children and I would live out creative dreams; we would paint, dance, run, sing and be a happy family all day long. Everyone would read and love reading. We would all know our times tables, and if an inspector ever came within earshot we would chirp them frontwards and backwards like a troupe of happy birds at dawn. We would apply them to quite complex everyday situations. I would be a hero in the community and would, possibly, stay there all my life, educating generations of children in my own special way.

'You'll get lonely and bored,' said Wes.

'They can be bloody difficult, those little rural communities, scared to spend money, scared to see anything change. After two years you'll still be an outsider,' said Alan.

They were right, which was why I ignored them and applied for the position of sole teacher, Scale A, at Papuni Primary School in the Hawke's Bay Education Board district. In those days, you had to do several years of country service. Papuni qualified. It was a sheep station on Māori incorporated land in the Upper Ruakituri Valley, which runs more or less parallel to the road from Wairoa to Lake Waikaremoana. The school was thirty-two kilometres due east from Lake Waikareiti, some seventy kilometres from the nearest shop but only fifty-two kilometres from the pub at Tiniroto.

I won the job, not that there would have been any other applicants. Alan announced my new appointment at the end-of-year prizegiving and all the assembled farmers and farmers' wives broke into wild applause. This was the second time I had heard this community applaud. The first was when the question of corporal punishment was discussed at a well-attended parents' meeting. Various opinions were expressed, then Alan stood up and said, 'In any school of mine, if a boy misbehaves he will be strapped, and strapped hard.' The audience clapped and cheered. Later, many fathers shook Alan by the hand and patted him on the back. There were understanding words and smiles — this is the way we do it, we don't shirk responsibilities.

I wasn't sure if they saw the prospect of a young teacher going to the wilds of Urewera country as not shirking responsibility, or an appropriate punishment, or both.

5.

I HIRED A SMALL TRUCK, and in late January loaded it with my possessions, mainly books, a stereo, records and teaching bits, and headed for Papuni. Wes came with me to make sure I didn't get lost and to bring the truck back. I did not have a vehicle of my own, and had not, perhaps, fully addressed the logistics of the shops being seventy kilometres away.

I was, as we bumped along the glorious road to Lake Waikaremoana, full of excitement, apprehension and misgiving. Reality, which did not include joking and philosophising with Wes, was about to arrive. And it did, in the form of Papuni Station. Grand hills, a beautiful river, a small group of houses, all miles and miles from anywhere. Other friends had gone to London, one even to New York. I was twenty-four and I had, on some romantic teaching whim, pointed my tugboat in a very strange direction.

When I had applied for the job, I hadn't understood that the school was located on the station — not just the school itself, but the two huts that constituted teacher accommodation.

Now I was concerned about what this might mean for my independence – and realised that this fear was justified when I first met the station manager, Sam.

Sam was a short, wide Māori man. He was a native speaker of te reo. His hands were huge, moulded, and injured by a lifetime of backcountry farming. He walked like a boxer already in the ring and prepared for whatever may happen next. I was told he had a beautiful singing voice, but I never heard it. What I did hear was his sense of right and wrong. He had expectations of people and was tough on those who didn't measure up. Many of those who didn't measure up were young station hands who had been placed with Sam by the Department of Social Welfare to be given a clearer sense of direction. I heard stories about what Sam's version of 'a sense of direction' could include.

Strangely, I think Sam and I could have been friends if I had been more mature. I quickly learned that people were afraid of him, so I saw it as my duty to stand against him, to demonstrate that I wasn't a station employee, to capitalise on everything the King's College regime had taught me. I had ridiculous arguments with him. One of these stands out. The school was in the centre of the station, about eight kilometres from the homestead and my hutstead. Every weekday morning I picked up two of Sam's grandchildren and two children who stayed with Rangi, the station cook, and drove the station's old Land Rover up the twisting, elevated gravel road to the school. One morning after I had been at Papuni for about six months, Sam said, 'I have had a complaint. The kids tell me you drive too fast and they bounce around in the back.'

I denied this, although I knew it was probably true, and argued for thirty minutes about his right to make such a complaint. I wanted the station workers, who were hanging around waiting for the day's 'orders', to hear me stand up to him. He looked at me and said, as he walked away, 'I am sixty years old today.' I nearly called out, 'Well, Happy Birthday then!' but managed to restrain myself. At the end of the day, I went to see him, apologised for not listening, and promised to drive more carefully. He looked at me for a long time, then said, 'I am often disappointed.' We didn't talk much after that, and I realised I had missed an opportunity. I was now firmly lined up with the anti-Sam brigade, i.e. everyone. People working on the station lapsed into the easy morality of will Sam approve or disapprove, will I be able to keep this from him? I could see the potential for disappointment.

I was the one who was disappointed the first time I cautiously drove the Land Rover to the school, which was about thirty metres from the road and up a rough track. It was about a week before the children were due to come back. Sprawled across the track was one of the large black bulls the station was fattening. It was more than large, with hind-quarters like a hippopotamus. I found an alternative route, steeper and with blackberries, and eventually arrived at this, my first school.

The grounds were really a hay paddock, and the school was really a one-room prefab. Horse manure dotted the grounds and paths like dark, smelly anthills. There was much to do. Inside, there was even more to do. The school had been repainted over the holidays, and the painters had protected all the resources, the books and the cuisenaire rods, the paint and the crayons, the chalk, the dusters and the drawing pins, by putting them in a huge pile in the middle of the room with a blanket over the top. I went outside, sat on an off-level bench, lit a cigarette and sighed. This was going to be hard work.

After five long, tedious days, however, the place was in reasonable shape. I knew where everything was and longed to show my handiwork to someone – if only there had been someone available. Each evening I would go back to my hut, go for a walk by the river, read, listen to music and wonder if I could cope with two years of this. One of my most pressing problems was the mindblowing, blowfly-attracting supply of mutton. When Sam had gone to the Education Board to ask for a school, he had promised to give the teacher half a sheep and half a bag of potatoes each week. I told him I didn't need it. He told me he never went back on his word. Until I became better organised, I would sneak out into the garden in the middle of the night to bury my stockpile of ageing meat.

ON THE FIRST Friday evening of the term, ten-year-old Des knocked on my door: 'You can come over to our house for a beer and TV, Steve said.'

I asked him many questions in my best schoolteacher manner and received many monosyllabic answers in return, before he gestured, with a wave of his head, that it was time for us to go. Steve's house was about four hundred metres away, across the horse paddock – a journey I was to make many times, always fearful of walking into a horse on pitch-dark rural nights. Steve greeted me at the door on that first evening, one hand offering a shake, the other a bottle of beer.

'Sorry, didn't bring anything. Didn't know I'd be going out,' I said.

He smiled a slow smile. He was not a big man, but broad-shouldered and wiry, with a tendency to lean forward, like the cowboys I had seen from upstairs in the Saturday matinees at the Kaikohe pictures. Had he been at the Kaikohe pictures, he would have had to sit downstairs. His handshake was not strong, but this would have been by choice – I could feel it as a hand of great power, the skin hardened and gnarled by outdoor work. Hands that had suffered small cuts and tears that had never been given enough time off to heal. Some lines from the poet Kathleen Raine raced into my mind: 'Shaped as they are by all life's restless cruelty / Forgiven, these hands must die'. I didn't think that Steve's hands needed to be forgiven, but they bore the signature of his work, as did my soft teaching hands.

These thoughts drifted around my head, making me a bit distracted when I met his wife, Josephine. More shy smiles and mumbled words. We didn't say much for the whole evening, hiding in the grainy black-and-white images that flickered over the TV screen. I did learn, however, that Steve was a shepherd, that he thought Sam was a bastard, that Josephine was going to have a baby and that Des was Josephine's little brother. It was a warm, awkward meeting, but I was so grateful to be there. I had no understanding of how close the three of us would become, how at home I would come to feel in their house.

Steve promised to give me a riding lesson the next day. A

city boy was about to become a country boy; a King's College, university boy was about to become a real New Zealander, or so I thought as I stumbled back across the horse paddock.

IN THE FIRST few weeks of school, possibly the whole of Term One, I knew I was not connecting with the kids. They were not disobedient or difficult, just passive and distant. School was something they had to do and they accepted that, but they would have preferred to ride their horses up the hills or catch the fat eels that thrived in the Ruakituri River. I worried a lot. It was my energy that was driving things. My tentative ideas about child-centred education and a creative classroom stayed on the runway, engines cold and still. Of course, a lot of this was because they found me a strange creature, looking and sounding so different from other adults in their lives.

That feeling of being strange had been evident even on my first school day, when I went to pick up the Land Rover from the yard dressed in my standard primary teacher summer gear – short-sleeved ironed shirt, tie, crimplene shorts and long walk socks. The sundry station hands in the yard stopped what they were doing and stared. 'Christ,' said one of them, 'seen better-looking legs on a crayfish!'

The running around and early morning art that had been so enthralling at Huapai didn't work at this school. The kids ran with feet firmly on the ground, no flying or twinkling or dancing. Their paintings were thin and drab. They were reluctant to talk about anything.

In time, things changed. They got to know me, heard stories about me falling off the horse Steve used when he was teaching me to ride, knew that the horse was the worst one on the station, and heard the rumour that I sometimes bumped into Sam's big horse when I walked home from Steve and Josephine's place — nobody really watches in tiny places like this, but everything is seen by someone. They started to enjoy the classical music I played on the school's remarkably good stereo every morning as I prepared for the day.

'Play the one that goes da-da-di-da, please.'

They would sing snatches of Ella Fitzgerald, Louis Armstrong, *Carmen* and my favourite Bach fugue. Mr L C M Saunders would have been proud of me.

The breakthrough, if that is the right word, came from the stories I read aloud. The children seemed suddenly able to 'hear' the stories and started to acknowledge their hunger for them. TV was not available in most homes and there was no way the kids could go to the pictures. Most were not fully independent readers and, even if they were, the school's supply of books was woeful, until I was able to hook into the fantastic Country Library Service. They wanted me to read 'chapter books' to have a story on the go. Just as the kids at Huapai worked so we could race round outside, these ones worked so that we could have story time. Their ages ranged from four to thirteen, but it didn't seem to matter. Each of them got whatever they got from the story, from sitting with the others, sharing an experience. We read all sorts of books. Kate Seredy's *The Good Master*, set on a large farm in Hungary, grabbed them straight away, as it did when my father read it to me. They were open-mouthed at *I Am David* by Anne Holm, and marvelled at its description of a boy who had grown up in the deprived environment of a concentration camp discovering an orange for the first time.

If there was one book to stand out, to define the experience for me, and I hope them, it was *Island of the Blue Dolphins* by Scott O'Dell. This is the story of a twelve-year-old American Indian girl and her little brother, stranded on an island off California in the 1800s. It is based on a true story. I remember one particular day. We had read several chapters, enough to get into the story and start wondering what would happen next. It was winter and Papuni is elevated enough to get snow. A traditional school pot-belly stove was blazing in the room — the older kids were great at lighting it, and Sam had provided a twenty-year supply of firewood. With the help of Rangi Tumanako, the station cook, a woman large in formidableness, stature and kindness, I had the usual winter pot of everything-imaginable-soup ready to heat up for lunch. The kids gathered around the stove, freezing, particularly those who had ridden to school on their horses. Guy, the boy everyone had told me was difficult, asked me to read the book, then and there, before nine o'clock. There was a chorus of enthusiasm, so I put aside thoughts of reading and maths, and started to read. Somehow I ended up, we ended up, reading all day. Reading, stoking the fire, chewing soup (it was that kind of soup) and reading until we finished the book.

I was, of course, scared that I would be found out: that the dreaded unexpected inspector would knock on the door and I would have to run away, as Janet Frame had done. I wondered what parents would think. Would Sam decide I was an unworthy teacher and stop giving me lumps of dead sheep? But more important than all these fears was the feeling that we had, somehow, become a family, that we were united by this snowy day, learning about the courage of an isolated girl in a place so much colder than ours. The sense of wonder about that magical day is still with me, and I hope it is, in some degree at least, with the little group of twelve children who were with me. The roll had been eighteen, but one family left the area, taking their six children with them. This was the beginning of the battle, acted out in so many rural schools, where declining roll numbers made closure a constant threat.

I don't think Papuni School cost the Education Board a lot. They didn't pay me very much. They did, however, pay the children two small allowances, one for cleaning the school, the other the famous chaff allowance to pupils who rode to school on horseback. I had to fill in a Chaff Allowance Return every term, and then distribute the ten shillings they each received. There were arguments about who should get the money if three members of a family came on the same horse.

These children could ride well, unlike me, despite Steve's promised lesson. He had taken me down to the stockyards and saddled up two horses, his looking lean and strong, mine a bit fat and wobbly. He showed me how to get on and off, making me do this twice. He then said, 'Follow me!' I had assumed we would do a couple of circuits of the stockyard and then have a chat about it, but three hours later I was still following him. My horse was slow, and it needed to trot to keep up: bump, bump, bump, up, down, up, down. I began to hate the horse, Steve and the whole bloody place.

Back at the stockyards, I got off, as instructed, and promptly fell over.

'Another lesson tomorrow?' smiled Steve.

'No thank you,' I replied.

It was perhaps the last time this level of politeness prevailed in our friendship.

It took days to recover from this lesson, but in many ways it had worked. I was never a good rider, but I could stay on a horse – mainly. The children, even the youngest, were confident, agile riders. On the days I rode to school, they would catch up with me on the road, then gallop ahead, turning to see how far behind I was, then they would circle back, full of laughter. They, of course, rode bareback, and I had my new saddle, purchased in Wairoa for ten pounds on a Friday evening with Steve as my adviser. It was an Officer's Saddle and I thought it was splendid, but when I came to leave I couldn't give it away.

I WAS OUT RIDING when I met four-year-old Huki. His father, King, was a shepherd, living at the back of the station. King's three older sons were at the school. His wife, Mary, had died the previous year. King told me that she had owned a car, a small Morris of some description. People in remote valleys like the Ruakituri know most of the vehicles that go up and down their road. They look up at the sound of an engine and say, There goes Old Fred again, or Rangi or the freight truck. King didn't want people to hear the car and mention his wife's name, so he buried the car with her.

After Mary died, Huki went to work with his father every day, sitting behind the saddle, hanging on through the equestrian complexity and brinkmanship that characterises a shepherd's day. Well, he was supposed to be hanging on, but people thought he had developed the skill of sleeping and somehow not falling off. King was a cheerful, tall-story-telling man. He always amused me, but I never knew what to believe. He maintained he would have been an All Black but he was so fast the dead ball line always came up too quickly for him to dot down the ball and score tries. He told me about the size of wild boars he had killed, the horses he had tamed and, at every meeting, his wife's car.

I told him to send Huki to school. Once the idea of looking after him came into my head, I had a growing fear of him sleeping and falling. I had no option but to take him. As it turned out, Huki was a memorable, cheerful member of our little class. In the first few weeks, however, he insisted on going outside to play in the mud. This drove his dad to such despair that one day he sent him to school in nappies: 'Just haven't got nothing else, Tim.' Huki hung around the door, reluctant to come in. He spent most of the day in the woodshed. Suffice it to say, he avoided mud thereafter.

I will forever remember him, if for no other reason than his enthusiasm for folk dancing. This was part of the New Zealand curriculum, and each school was issued with a set of 45 EP records and an instruction manual. I have always found that after initial reluctance, children enjoy folk dancing. At Papuni we would clear away the desks and tables, turn up the music as loud as possible, and skip, yell and do-si-do to 'Oh! Susanna' and 'Red River Valley', big kids and little kids together, having exuberant fun and developing considerable skill.

Whenever Huki saw me getting out the records, he would yell 'Yippee, folking dance!' The others delighted in this — it was as risqué as school life got in 1966. It also let me know that school was perceived as a different place with different values from those of their everyday lives. Their parents swore often and loudly. They swore themselves, but school was not a place for swearing and I tried to avoid doing so, despite the many moments of despair.

Often, in the afternoon, Huki would go to sleep, sitting on the lap of one of the two Form Two girls, Charlotte and Hinekorako. For this to happen seemed natural and uncomplicated. It was my first real introduction to the notion of tuakana-teina, the Māori concept of older children looking after younger ones, a concept that was to become so important in my later ideas about family grouping. Mind you, I did hear opposition to this concept, such as when Huki became cross with Hinekorako and said: 'You think you can boss me around jus' 'cos you've got big tits!'

Unexpectedly, the school was well equipped with gymnastics gear: a vaulting horse and stool, a small rebounder and some good thick mats. I didn't know much about gymnastics, but we would clear the room, set up the gear and, as they say, give it a go. It was a mixture of fun and crashes, both of them a tribute to the children's backcountry resilience. I wanted to teach them the vault I remembered from my own schooldays — we knew it as a long vault or long fly. It involved racing up to the horse, diving along its full length and, at the last possible second, planting hands on the very end to gain enough elevation for spread legs to be in the clear and the vaulter to head for the mat, with varying degrees of elegance. As with most vaults, it required speed, courage and either commitment or foolishness. The kids at Papuni were not getting it, so I decided I would demonstrate. I positioned them near the landing area, with instructions to steady me if I lost control. Needless to say, when they saw me flying through the air they did swift calculations — speed times weight equals velocity — and it was obviously sensible to stand clear. I crashed into the back wall, making a teacher-sized hole. Over the next few days most of them surreptitiously wrote 'Sir did this!' around the hole. I was, heaven help me, still Sir.

I knew that everyone on the station would quickly hear of this incident, and construe it as either courage or another example of my lack of rural virtues, but what surprised me was how far the story travelled. Steve and I were in a bar in Wairoa when the barman found out we were from Papuni and said, 'So, you the blooody teacher, then, tried to knock down the bloody walls of the bloody school.' He laughed but didn't offer a free beer, which I thought was the least he could do.

The vaulting, the folk dancing and other games kindled the kids' appetite for physical activity. More than that, it gave one or two of them who found learning difficult something they could shine at. Billy, quiet, slow and possibly knocked around at home, became a vaulting hero, ultimately able to dive the full length of the horse and land with a forward roll on the mat at the far end. When we had an end-of-year parents' day, he demonstrated this skill and everyone, especially his dad, was enthralled.

One of my reasons for loving outdoor activities with kids — exercise, sports and camps — is that so often students who gain no mana for their performance in the classroom can unexpectedly display outstanding skills and attitudes. Watching Billy reinforced, for me, my responsibility as a teacher to find a way for every child to excel at something. Sadly, this can be difficult to bring about. The truth of the cynical observation 'To those who have, more shall be given' is borne out time and time again. Many kids seem to go through school without receiving anything to make them feel good about themselves. Good teachers find something and reward it, make a little rain fall in every desert.

MY CONTACT WITH other people in the area greatly increased after I purchased a 1948 Ford V8 pickup truck. It was small, with a narrow cab, it had holes in the floor, it made smoke, it didn't like hills, and it consumed petrol as if it was fully confident the price would never go above a dollar a gallon. But it was the best vehicle I could have bought, because so many people up and down the valley had owned one. People with whom it would have been too hard to start a conversation would talk easily about the Ford V8 engine, its virtues and its iniquities.

But much of my life at Papuni centred around Steve. He taught me to ride, in my fashion. He also took me hunting

74

for deer and pigs. It seemed that hunters coming in from the Waikaremoana Road drove game towards the western boundary of the station, making animals reasonably plentiful. Steve had been in the bush most of his life, and was fit and strong. I struggled to keep up with him. One of his favourite tricks, when I lagged behind, was to double back through the bush, silent and invisible, then come up behind me, poke his rifle in my back and say, 'Lucky we're not in Vietnam, eh?' He found this more amusing than I did.

We took horses and rifles when hunting for deer, and could sell everything we killed to the meat-exporting agency that had a depot at the Tiniroto pub. Head- or neck-shot deer fetched, as soon as decimal currency was introduced, 13 cents a pound; body-shot deer, 10 cents. We thought these were excellent prices and aimed to take two or three carcases in every week — all, well nearly all, head-shot. The placing of the freezer next to the pub was a strategic move and we seldom came home with all we got paid.

Pigs were a different proposition. We had little sympathy for them, especially when we came across evidence of their killing and eating of newborn lambs. Contrary to the conventional image of pigs, the New Zealand wild pig is an athletic animal, fast, cunning and strong. Its tusks can inflict serious damage with casual ease. Either out of foolhardiness or overconfidence, we would chase pigs through the bush armed only with Steve's dogs and our knives. Rifles were an encumbrance in the bush, and we didn't want to endanger the dogs by shooting into the confusion of dogs and prey. Old hunters in the pub would praise what we were able to bring in, but warned us that injury was inevitable. 'One day, boys, one day your guard will be down a bit, or you'll slip, or you'll meet a real nasty bugger. One day, mark my words.'

The thought of 'one day' was pushed to the back of our minds and we basked in our success. We were flattered when people at the marae in Te Rēinga, a small settlement on the inland road between Wairoa and Gisborne, would ring up and ask us to get a pig for forthcoming social events.

Once, we were sitting around Rangi's place on a snowy day, playing cards and drinking.

'You reckon you boys could get us a little piggy for dinner?' Rangi asked.

'Course,' we said.

We assembled the dogs, always excited at the prospect of a hunt, and grabbed a horse to take us across the river to the steep bush-covered slopes of our favourite hunting area. However, before we reached the river we spotted an ideal little pig that had strayed onto our side of the river. It was quickly grabbed by the dogs and despatched. We built a big fire, partly to keep warm but mainly so we could singe the pig. This done, we triumphantly went back to Rangi's — the whole operation had taken less than an hour. This became another story that circulated far more widely than it should have, the size of the pig increasing and the time taken to get it decreasing with every telling.

It was a cruel business. The dogs had the task of holding the pig until we arrived. We would then grab it under the jaw, tip its head back and thrust a knife down its neck in the general direction of its heart. I cannot believe I did this, but I did, with relish and without conscience.

Sometimes, the pigs got their own back. One afternoon we toiled uphill towards the sound of the dogs on what seemed like a big mob of pigs. There were too many for the dogs to hold, and pigs raced downhill in our direction, their squealing reaching demonic proportions. Just when they broke, I was negotiating my way under a large tangle of fallen supplejack. My negotiation was not very effective and I ended up on my stomach with one boot raised behind me, firmly locked in a tangle of vine. I lay there as the fleeing pigs charged through the supplejack on their way to freedom, some giving a toss of their tusks as they flashed past — not close enough to injure but close enough for bad dreams. However, pride, overconfidence and adrenalin prevented us from learning from experience. We rushed downhill after them and found that the dogs had managed to hold two in a hole that had been formed when a huge tree had fallen. Without hesitation, we leapt in, bowling pigs over as we landed, grabbing them and killing them. Steve and I hauled ourselves out of the hole, dragging the pigs with us, then we lay on the muddy ground and laughed and laughed, with only a small touch of hysteria.

The pigs did have a small posthumous revenge. When you carry a pig out of the bush, you get your mate to lift it onto your back with its front legs straddling your neck, its head nodding beside yours and its dead eyes looking ahead. You hold on to its feet, and the muscly front thighs rest comfortably on your shoulders. To the casual observer, this positioning of the pig almost makes it look as if it has won the battle and is enjoying the spoils of conflict. As the pig's body cools, the multitude of lice it has hosted crawl onto your warm neck and down your warm back. Lice, pig's blood, sweat, mud and, as often as not, our own blood combined to make us unpleasant to be near. Josephine wouldn't let Steve in the house until he'd washed under the garden hose. He advised me against marriage.

There were many other adventures, like the time we stayed out too late and the darkness of mythical nights descended on the bush. Steve took off one of his gumboots, placed it on a stick and set it alight. It flared and spat and smoked, but gave us enough light to see the track. Unfortunately, small pieces of molten rubber kept falling off the boot, starting little fires on our clothing.

On another day, we took only one horse, Flicka, to get us across the river. Somehow, a dog ran under and around Flicka, dragging a chain that wound around her legs. Flicka, the nicest and most tolerant of horses, began to buck wildly. Steve, sitting in front of me, fell sideways. I felt myself going high in the air as Flicka lifted her hindquarters so she could kick the chain off her legs. I was still, technically, on the horse, but I knew my arms and legs were spread as wide as possible as some instinct instructed me that this was the best way to maintain balance. And it was, for a few seconds, before we parted company and I began what might have been a graceful arc that ended in the mud beside Steve. We were unable to stand for several minutes, not because of injury but because we were, again, laughing too hard. We laughed, the kids who were watching laughed, and people down the road laughed when the story spread with that magical speed of rural rumour and scuttlebutt.

After we had been hunting together for about eight months, the pigs had a significant victory. The dogs had, again, found a big mob. They had been unable to hold such a large number and, in the ensuing struggle, half the pigs raced in one direction, hotly pursued by half the dogs. Steve gave a yell and chased one lot, indicating I should follow the other. At the best of times, it was hard for our dogs to do their job properly — they were Steve's sheep dogs, excellent at gentle herding, but while they seemed to enjoy the thrill and rough and tumble of the chase this was not what they had been bred for. Their effectiveness was in numbers. When there were three of them to every pig, they could hold it and subdue it. On this occasion, dogs and pigs had scattered. I caught up with a single dog trying valiantly to bail a pig up in a mud hole. I raced in to grab it, but it was more or less free to fight back, and somehow my hand that was supposed to go under its chin ended up in its mouth. It did as all good pigs should and chomped down in a rolling, grinding kind of a way. I let out a shriek loud and shrill enough for the pig to wonder if we were related.

I clutched my hand, the pig scrambled out of the hole, and the dog lay in the mud, looking disgusted. I washed my bruised and bleeding hand in a nearby creek, and it didn't seem too bad. I couldn't move all of my fingers, but I ascribed that to the bruising. When Steve arrived, dragging two small pigs, he helped me wrap up my hand in his overlarge, possibly overused, country handkerchief. We chased a few more pigs, unsuccessfully, and then went home. It was our habit to finish a hunt sitting on the back steps of my hut, ideally in the sunshine, drinking a glass or two of the cheap whisky we told ourselves we had totally earned. We used some of the whisky to clean up and sterilise the hand, and the rest as a necessary anaesthetic now that the adrenalin and excitement had faded.

The school holidays started in a week, so I thought I would wait until I was back in Auckland before seeking medical treatment. It doesn't pay to injure yourself if you live in the backblocks. All that needs to be said is that today my left hand functions quite well, thanks to the skill of several surgeons. They replaced the severed tendons with wire and ultimately removed the little finger. It had responded to the abuse by curling up into a ball and generally being a nuisance.

The most interesting thing about this is that when I go into a classroom full of children for the first time, they immediately notice the missing finger and comment on it. As one little guy said: 'You've got only four hands.' Adults, with one important exception, tend not to notice. The exception is poets, who notice almost as quickly as children – ponder that!

MORE QUICKLY THAN I thought possible, the end of my second year at Papuni loomed. The school was humming along nicely, and I had the daily joy of hearing new readers celebrate their achievement. I also had the worry of one little girl, Sam's granddaughter Amy, not quite getting it yet. My confident reassurances that she would were sounding a bit thin both to the grandparents and to me. I was at a loss, just as I am years later when I encounter kids for whom reading seems a step too far.

I have long thought that most parents are brilliant when their children are learning to talk. There is usually no real pressure for it to happen too soon, and there is little direct teaching. First efforts are received with enthusiasm and praise, and errors are celebrated. The child is allowed to work her or his own way through the huge array of data all around them. We are different when it comes to reading. There are expectations, errors are pounced on, and there is a sense that the child must hurry lest they fall behind their chronological peers. Of the many things I learned at Papuni, the greatest and most influential was that chronological age does not indicate what a child can or cannot do, should or should not do. I came to believe that the most secure learning happens when a child is ready, and that our expectations of the unready can be deeply damaging.

At the end of my second year, I knew I had to leave. It would have been great to stay, but, despite the people I had come to know, despite the huge fun Steve and I had chasing animals up and down hills, I was lonely, socially and professionally. I needed other teachers; I needed a companion.

The wretched grading system had managed to make its way to the wilds of Papuni. On the day an inspector was due, there had been a slip on the road. The only way to get to the school was on horseback. I waited at the gate with several children and a spare horse, and when the inspector arrived we told him it was horseback or nothing. He was delighted with the experience and the story he was clearly going to be able to tell his colleagues. The day had a picnic atmosphere, and I knew I would get top marks.

I spent Christmas 1966 at the marae at Te Rēinga. It was a long party that somehow became a New Year's-long party. It was good boozy comfortable fun, but I knew I had to leave, had to become a city boy again.

I had bought, as you did, a Mini, resplendent in English racing green, capable of hurtling around tight gravel corners in a spectacular way, inhibited only by a tendency for its little bottom to scrape on the road. It, like me, was meant for tarsealed roads. I had given Steve the pickup, which was only fair considering that his mechanical skills had kept it alive.

One morning I said farewell words to everyone.

'I'm off, then,' I said to Steve.

'Yeah, time to go,' he replied.

We shook hands, perhaps more warmly than the first time. I jumped in the Mini and headed for Auckland, tears in my eyes, optimism in my heart.

I never saw any of these people again. A few years ago, I drove to Papuni to look at the little school that was the source of so many big ideas. It had gone – the walls, the roof, the floor the kids and I polished by hand, the wood burner, the artwork and the books. The only thing remaining was the small, inadequate hole-in-the-ground toilet.

I had Ozymandias thoughts, but decided they were too grandiose.

6.

I WON A new job at Beresford Street School in Central Auckland. It was exactly the job I wanted. The school was — and 'was' is the correct word in that it no longer exists — in the inner-city suburb of Freemans Bay. The buildings remain — they have been assimilated by Auckland Girls' Grammar. Today's children go to the new and expanding Freemans Bay School, built on the site of the old Napier Street School. One trusts that the old rivalry between Napier Street and Beresford Street no longer exists, and the posturing and yelling that was part of going home has long gone.

Freemans Bay, in the 1960s, was not fashionable. It had a stock of magnificent houses, most in need of general repair and the upgrading of back-of-the-house kitchens and bathrooms that reflected Victorian values. Kitchens were the domain of women and servants, so ventilation, light, size and convenience did not need to be considered. Bathrooms deserved little mention apart from a sense of wonder that came if they were actually inside.

People from the Pacific were arriving in New Zealand in large numbers, some with the necessary documentation, some without, many with it only to find their legitimacy doubted by officials. They came to Freemans Bay and the neighbouring suburbs of Ponsonby and Grey Lynn, where rents and purchase prices were low. They came because it was likely that someone from their home village would live nearby. They came because there were churches where they could be harangued in their own languages, have a tenth of their low income taken and fill the early Sunday morning air with gloriously harmonious singing.

Their children came to us, to Beresford Street School, to me, for the education they had left their homelands for. I had been teaching Māori children at Papuni, and I had seen how the system had failed many of them and their families. There is a sense of disillusion that comes when people know there is not necessarily a pot of gold for them at the end of the educational rainbow. Pacific Island children, and their families, still believed there was. It was our job, my job, to help them get their hands on the pot.

I turned up for the first day of meetings clad in my crayfish-legs outfit but minus a tie. I was excited to be working with other teachers, to be with people who understood, who had ideas. I remembered, as I do to this day, what Steve had said to me when we met for a beer one Friday evening, as was our habit. I had had a difficult week at school, and felt that no one, least of all me, had made any progress.

'What did you do today, mate?' I asked.

'I built a gate,' he replied, with a matter-of-fact casualness that indicated he didn't realise the effect this answer had on me. It must be a glorious feeling to have such a tangible result for your day's work — something to hold, touch, show to others. Something to swing on.

Now I sat in the Beresford Street staffroom, eager and ready, a bit shy, but with gate-builder written all over me. The acting principal, John, asked to have a word outside.

'The tie, Tim, did you forget it? Know it's just a teachers' day but we need to keep up standards, you know. Standards.'

He was not a bad man, but he was a gate-closer. He liked me, wanted to be on-side with me, but he also restricted me in his desire to have enough paperwork to cover any possible questions. The shorthand planning that had been sufficient at Papuni was not enough — one of the many positives about a sole-charge school is that communication between teacher and principal is usually quick and straightforward.

John had fought in the Korean War and patriotism burned fiercely in his heart, all the more so when occasional palpitations and dizzy spells suggested all was not well. He loved school assemblies, which he tried to run with the precision of King's College military drill. Several times he became hugely upset at the children's failure to take things seriously and to march with any kind of recognition of left right, left right. The special-class children with their tendency to chant 'left-right-left-right' while swinging both arms in parallel arcs filled him with despair.

At one particular assembly he became very worked up, yelling about honouring his dead comrades, and about how in New Zealand we knew the value of the flag and if they were going to live here they needed to do likewise. Another young teacher, and lifelong friend, Tim Haslett, and I needed to take him by the arms and lead him away, citing stress on his heart as the reason. This wasn't the real reason, but his sweating, shaking limbs, racing pulse and face drained of colour suggested it was a very good one. To die trying to shape up a school assembly may not have qualified for special recognition from the RSA, but it was something he risked day after day.

I came to realise that he didn't read the planning material he demanded beyond a quick look to see that there were enough pages. This freed me to submit the same set of lesson plans every week, the new date printed large and persuasively in the top corner. I started each week armed with a few notes, enough to get things up and running, and a belief that we needed to be flexible enough to pursue interests, and needs, as they developed.

I had been given the 'language class'. This contained children John decided had the greatest need for extra English tuition. The roll at the beginning of the year was small, and was to be added to as new children arrived from the Pacific. They were of a variety of ages and needs — John felt my sole-charge experience would allow me to cope with this unusual arrangement. He was right, and this fitted my growing belief that chronological age has very little significance in what a child can and cannot do. I knew very little about what was then called Teaching English as a Second Language, so resolved to just teach and believe that language gains would follow, and proceeded to have as much fun as possible. I also awaited the arrival of the newly appointed principal, Pius Blank. I was delighted with the rumours about him being an unconventional forward-thinker.

I enjoyed the company of Tim Haslett, who was in the school for a term with the task of improving maths teaching. We played in the same rugby team. We discomforted some of the staff with our jokes, horseplay and ferocious games of padder tennis. We organised equally ferocious games for the senior boys, in the hope that this would let off some of the energy John would try to strap out of them.

My language class was slow to accept me and my ways. It seemed that they had a fear of doing something wrong and so were passive followers. Certainly, they could be exuberant in the playground and loud in the classroom, but they looked to me to lead them and were a long way from being in contact with their childhood, with the things that they might be able to make or express. I became a slightly demented Pied Piper as I tried to lead them back to themselves, daring them to be children.

The answer, once again, lay in art. Even as I write it, I know this is the wrong word. It is the convenient title given to an array of activities involving paint, paper, water, glue, brushes, feathers, clay, crayons and all manner of found objects. It involved telling children that what they wanted to do was the right thing, that there was no best way, and that, providing they worked hard and seriously, I would love the result. We ended up with the swirls and whorls and eruptions of colour from their Pacific Island homes. Inevitably, the angles, straight lines and muted pallet of their new home started to be included. Slowly, they started to trust me with their spontaneity, fears and dreams. Slowly, John started to accept what I was doing, even if it happened at what should have been arithmetic time.

I often took them into the centre of the city. This involved a short walk up the hill to Pitt Street and then catching the famous Farmers free bus to Queen Street. We did this so often that the drivers started to question our right to be there: 'This bus is for people shopping at Farmers, not joy-riding kids.'

I pointed out that their parents did a lot of shopping, that they would grow up to be shoppers, none of which was very persuasive. What did work was the kids talking to the drivers, as I encouraged them to do:

'Good afternoon, Mr Bus Driver, Sir. May I sit on your bus?'

'Thank you, Mr Driver, for steering this canoe so safely.'

'May God bless you, your family and your wheels.'

This, and their songs and their chatter, became our *pasese*, our fare.

On these outings I could see their enthusiasm growing or, more accurately, being released. We would read street signs, shop names and the multitude of instructions that decorate our streets. They would rush ahead of me to find new signs to read in the sing-song chant they had learned in the overly large classrooms of their homelands. Passersby would help, trying to ensure the 'b' of 'bus stop' was not pronounced as a 'p' and the oddities of 'th' were not glossed into a 'd'.

One day I took two of them in my car to the university. I had a lot of books to return to the library and I wanted them to help carry them. I also thought it would be a nice adventure. As we neared the university it became clear they were terrified.

'Will there be any students?' they asked. Students, for them, were the rioters they had seen on television, clashing with police and property.

Remarkably, no one became lost or got run over on these excursions. If I were to do the same thing today, I would need to recruit adult helpers. I would need to fill out forms, including one assessing the risks I didn't want to know about. Risks? The kids at Papuni took huge risks when they jubilantly dived over the vaulting horse; everyone took risks when they ran as fast as they could, or climbed high or tackled a big kid. I hope I was never reckless, but I lament how careful, how risk-averse, how boring our schools have had to become.

At the beginning of Term Two, the new principal, Pius Blank, arrived. He immediately gave me encouragement, freedom, friendship and a few beers after school on Friday. It was the beginning of a long, and at times complex, friendship. Perhaps the time at Beresford Street School was the best of this friendship – when we were young, and full of optimism. Pius will return several times in this story and I will document the difficulties he and I had. What is important here is that, in 1968, he was the friend and mentor I needed.

Pius thought my approach to art was amusing but justified. He made sure I had all the materials I needed. Under his leadership, assemblies were abandoned and military music no longer rang across the suburb at nine in the morning; male staff wearing ties became optional, and planning could be recorded in a minimal way.

John, his predecessor, lasted the term, disillusioned, dispirited and given to making statements that revealed some deep-seated prejudices. He died shortly afterwards, the heart that he said would race whenever he strapped someone perhaps deciding none of it was worth the effort any more.

IN MARCH OF my first year at Beresford Street I enrolled in the Masters course in Social Anthropology at Auckland University. This was going to involve sitting four papers and completing a thesis. I was excited by the prospect of returning to formal studies, and believed I could fit the demands of the course around my teaching, rugby and social life. It is amazing how much time is available when you don't own a house and have lawns to mow, cabbages to water and windows to fix. A staff member who lived near the school tried to persuade me to buy a house in the area while they were still dead cheap. She was convinced that their value would increase and that I would never regret the decision. I didn't believe her. Time proved her right and me very wrong!

On the day of my first lecture I announced at morning tea, as casually as I could, that I was driving to university after school and would be happy to give anyone who needed it a lift. A young Sāmoan woman on the staff, Fuatino Ainiusami Matalavea, Siainiu for short, more or less smiled that she would appreciate a lift. She always wore a traditional Sāmoan *puletasi* and seemed to glide rather than walk. She was not tall but held herself in a way that seemed lofty, even haughty. Her command of English was regal, precise or colloquial as the occasion demanded. I think she was the first truly bilingual person I had ever met. It came as no surprise to learn that she had been sent on a scholarship from the remote village of Safune, on Savai'i, to the Third Form at St Mary's College in Taranaki. People from Anglican private schools can recognise each other and, although we hadn't really talked, we had exchanged some nods of understanding, especially when John had mangled the language.

That lunchtime I tidied my car up a bit.

The journeys to university happened every Tuesday and Thursday, and although I never really tidied up the car again, I looked forward to them and to the increasing time we spent that was neither travelling nor attending lectures. However, this book is supposed to be about teaching, so I shall not discuss these adventures, wonderful as they were, beyond saying that six months later we were married. Married, living at beautiful Cheltenham Beach, awaiting our first child and full of excited optimism, fools that we were.

It would be wrong to say she was the girl I dreamed of in my lonely times at Papuni. Siainiu had qualities and strengths beyond the world I knew; she had so much to teach me. The popular perception was, and probably still is, that if you marry into a Pasifika family, they will drain you of all your financial and emotional resources. My experience has been the opposite. Her vast extended family, for the many years I have known them, have treated me with extraordinary kindness and patience. Having said that, I do have to confess to some impatience when Siainiu and I walked together down Karangahape Road or through the Ōtara shopping centre. She kept meeting family, or people from her village, or people she didn't really know but who had recognised her as Sāmoan. Each of these encounters involved laughter, perhaps tears, hand-holding, animated discussion and a quite extraordinary consumption of time.

Marriage enhanced my teaching. More accurately, my energy for teaching and my language class bounced along happily with me. We took on ambitious art projects involving large paintings and very messy batik-making. After a ferry trip to Devonport, we painted a ferryboat picture that took up the entire back wall of the classroom. This was a huge task and I marvelled at how the class became determined to finish it. I also marvelled at how those who took on leadership roles were not the ones I expected to do so. The students seemed to be able to recognise those with skills and were prepared to be guided by them.

I was learning, far more slowly than I should, that children left alone can often perform at levels well beyond conventional expectation. I came to realise that it is a teacher's responsibility to set boundaries, to supply materials and some guidance, and to believe that children who know that their natural creativity is trusted and welcomed can do wonderful things. It is a great sadness to see how much we do to undermine their trust in this creativity. How many times do teachers 'show' children how to paint, hold up samples of the 'right' way to make a picture, and use creative activities as time-fillers at the fag end of the day? Here I make a plea for the abolition of colouring-in books for children, books that say this is how it is done.

I like to think I was able to dare the kids in my language class to be kids, and unleash creative energy that owed something to both their original homes and this confusing city their families had brought them to. I also think working in this way helped their learning of English, in that they felt compelled to talk. We did some regular lessons, chanted words and poems, wrote something every day, talked about oddities like spelling and apostrophes. I don't think these things helped as much as the need to persuade someone that they wanted the side of the ferryboat to be a different colour.

I would gaze around the mess of my room and the kids working so intently that it didn't matter if I was there or not, and feel a special contentment. This was how I wanted to teach, how I felt I should teach. Little did I know that this would be the last class I would work with in this way.

OUR DAUGHTER, PENELOPE Sasao, was born in March the following year, 1969. Her name was carefully chosen. We believed Penelope could be pronounced, without trouble, by both English and Sāmoan speakers. I loved the lilt of the Sāmoan articulation of every vowel: Pe-ne-lo-pe. The name, however, became shortened to Lope, which has served her well, all the way to her current position as a District Court judge. Sasao was her maternal grandmother's name and refers to the coming of the volcanic eruption of Mt Matavanu, in Savai'i in 1905, a famous and fitting name — not that I think volcanic eruption would be helpful on the Bench, although knowledge that it is a possibility might be.

It would be right to say my cup was overflowing — marriage, fatherhood, teaching and study, all of which I loved, were filling my time beyond my capabilities, and I knew something had to give. I stopped playing rugby, which left me feeling a bit twitchy on Saturday afternoons, but this didn't really save much time — I had been in a team that never practised, so the only commitment had been to the eighty minutes of playing and the many more minutes of socialising.

I did not want to give up my studies. I had become deeply interested in social anthropology, and while I didn't think getting an MA would help my career, it might allow me to catch up, a bit, to my brother Chris, who was just finishing his second doctorate. Ah, there are so many reasons to study. I had become ambitious, partly at Siainiu's prodding, partly from new dreams about running my own school. After lots of talk, we decided the best thing to do was for me to stop teaching halfway through the year and become a full-time student. I told Siainiu we would be as poor as church mice. She was thoughtful about religion, but it had a grip on her, as it has on the majority of Sāmoans, and she responded by saying church mice were in fact rich because of where they lived. Armed with this thought, I became a full-time student.

Pius was upset with me taking leave. I knew he had come to depend on me in the school. I could take rugby teams and take the older boys for long runs in the adjacent, and glorious, Western Park. I was also a kindred spirit, and, I think, in the isolation that can beset principals amid a multitude of trivia and disillusionment, a kindred spirit becomes invaluable. Pius came from the German-speaking region of Switzerland. His knowledge of English was far superior to my knowledge of any other language, but he did, much to my delight, make some errors with colloquialisms. My favourite was when he wanted to know how busy I was – i.e. my availability for an extra task.

'Well, Tim,' he would say, 'how flat are you out?'

I became totally flat out at university but loved the freedom, the privilege, of full-time study. I came to understand how study can be a joy and, for the first time in my life, gave it my all.

Siainiu and I talked endlessly about what to do after I had

sat my exams. One obvious option was to continue working at Beresford Street School, but we kept coming back to the notion of going to Sāmoa. There would be many advantages – it would be a great place for me to write my thesis, there would be child-minding relatives available to look after Lope while Siainiu went back to work, and there would be the feeling of doing something worthwhile.

The idea excited me, so we wrote to Sāmoa's Director of Education, Dr Faanafi Larkin, and offered our services. Faanafi was the first Sāmoan woman to gain a PhD, earned from the London School of Economics. The nation was proud of her and had high expectations. She clearly had high expectations of us. She wrote back offering me the position of principal at Palauli Junior High School. Siainiu was offered a teaching job at the school, but we quickly negotiated for her to become deputy principal. I was twenty-eight and had been teaching for five years – did I feel confident I could run a junior high school of about 250 students in another country? I feel both proud and ashamed that my answer was an emphatic yes.

Faanafi wrote back expressing delight at our acceptance but asked me if I wanted to be paid an expatriate salary or local salary, which was about 50 per cent smaller. Could I accept being paid twice as much as the woman I had married and with whom I had a child? No, I told Faanafi, expecting her to be pleased and full of praise. These things were expressed in her return letter, but what stood out was her message that teachers on local salary had to pay their own fares. To those who have . . .

7.

WE PACKED UP what little we owned and had it loaded on the ship *Wainui*. Little did we know that an industrial dispute would mean the ship would not move anywhere until August of the following year. Siainiu, Lope and I went by air. There were no direct flights to Western Sāmoa, and large planes had to land in Pagopago in American Sāmoa; from there we caught a DC3 to Faleolo. I have always regarded the DC3 as the hero, or heroine, of aviation passenger transport. About a month after we arrived in Apia, the hero, or heroine, we had travelled in crashed on take-off, with total loss of life. It ended up implanted vertically in the lagoon beside the airport, where it stayed for months, a stark reminder of the fragility of air travel.

On arrival we were met by Siainiu's brother Taimalie, a warm, kind, intelligent man who taught science at the Apia Teachers' College. He, like his sister, had been sent to New Zealand at a young age. He became a pupil at Southwell School in Hamilton and later New Plymouth Boys' High and

Ardmore Teachers' College. He succeeded at these places socially, academically and on the sports field. Sadly, New Zealand also taught him to drink alcohol, an enthusiasm he never learned to fully control. On this, my first day in Sāmoa, he took me to sundry clubs, and we drank more than even my training at the Astor Hotel had prepared me for. We made a late-night visit to Vailima, the Head of State's residence, a magnificent house built by Robert Louis Stevenson. Our enthusiasm for this visit was not matched by that of those on guard duty, and we were both arrested. I quickly learned that much in Sāmoa depends on who you know, and shortly afterwards we were un-arrested.

Siainiu was not impressed.

We stayed several days in Apia with Siainiu's friend Vaifou, whose house was next to Vaisigano School, where she was principal. I needed a shower and was taken to a square concrete room in the school. A water pipe came out of the wall, and from it issued a heavy stream of cold water. I smiled, remembering what Siainiu had told me before we left, when I was peppering her with questions about life in Sāmoa: 'I can tell you that having a shower under a cold tap is not a pleasant experience, even on the hottest of days, but you won't be able to fully believe or appreciate this until it happens.' I did not smile when a huge centipede ran across the floor. It was electric blue, a colour that spoke of poison and evil. I dried myself on an off-white towel and realised I had so much to learn.

Vaifou wanted to help me learn. She introduced me to her educational and child-raising philosophy, which seemed to be based on notions of Original Sin. As she put it, 'Children are full of shit and it's our duty to beat it out of them.'

She would not flinch from this duty and I could not persuade her away from it. How a person who was so kind and loving to us could flail around with a broom, or a jandal, when she perceived disobedience in very young children was something I never came to understand or accept. I floated ideas of compassion and reward, but these were sunk on the sharp rocks of her biblical beliefs. Damned missionaries, I thought, not for the first or last time.

About a week later we were taken in a Ministry of Works truck to the wharf at Faleolo to wait for the boat to take us to Saleloga, Savai'i's main port. Port might be the wrong word. It was more a navigable lagoon with a small wharf. The wait was long. The boat would not leave until there were enough passengers, and there was no knowing how long this would take. I had been told about this, too, and had thought it romantic, but the reality was very different.

After several hours, we got under way and began the two-hour lurch across the open sea between the two islands. The boat was really what I would have called a launch. We sat on the hatch, getting our feet wet on a deck that was frequently inundated when the roll of the boat invited the ocean to sluice down it. There was a prevailing smell of copra, cockroaches, tropical heat, diesel, and the vomit of the sons and daughters of the great Polynesian navigators. Locally, these boats were called *va'a kelosene* – kerosene boats – which seemed about right. I was told not to worry, despite the apparent lack of progress and my wet feet. Apparently, it was only when the locals started singing hymns that worry was justified.

At Saleloga we piled into another truck and were taken on the sixteen-kilometre journey to the village of Vaito'omuli, where the school was located. There was a house there for us, one of those the New Zealand government had built for New Zealand teachers. This was before the Agreement of Cooperation between the New Zealand and Sāmoan Departments of Education broke down. The agreement specified that teachers in a struggling undeveloped nation should be paid more than they would in a comfortable developed nation.

When we drove across the school grounds I received two mindblowing shocks. The first was the state of the house. Siainiu and I deemed it unliveable. We decided we should commandeer the truck and get the driver to take her and Lope to her parents' village, Safune, on the other side of the island, and I would return to Apia and explain our plight to anyone who would listen.

The second shock was, perhaps, more profound. Years before, in a fit of student curiosity, I had been with Eseta to see a fortune-teller, a dusty-looking woman who lived in the back streets of Kingsland, itself a very back-streets suburb at the time. The woman said she would read my aura and told me she saw a series of long, low buildings with wire netting covering the windows. We laughed afterwards at my being destined to become a chicken farmer. But I did not laugh when I looked at the school buildings. They matched her description with uncanny accuracy. Perhaps I was meant to be here. Perhaps the fortune-teller had had some knowledge of Sāmoan educational architecture and had picked me as a potential principal.

I caught a boat back to Faleolo. I was lucky in that it was almost full when I arrived and it was the best in the fleet, named *Taumafai*, which translates, in honour of Captain Cook, as 'Endeavour'. As we neared the wharf I wondered what I was going to do next. I knew I had to catch a bus but didn't know which one. Heat, tiredness and general confusion were robbing me of coherent thought, and I decided I would run around yelling 'Apia! Apia!' until someone pointed me in the right direction.

I didn't have to, because Taimalie was there waiting for me. He'd had a hunch that I might have to return and be rescued. My relief and gratitude were huge. Many years later, I told this story at his funeral, comparing my journey with his, and how I didn't know that somebody would be waiting for me, but that he, as a true believer, would know who was waiting for him. Hypocritical, perhaps, but it went down well.

I was directed to the senior inspector, Maiava. He listened to my tale of woe, told me he already knew of the situation, and had issued instruction for the local *matai*, or village chief, to repaint the house and replace all the mosquito netting on the windows. The work was already under way, and, in the meantime, he had arranged for us to stay with the pastor, Seilala, in the next village, its name a celebration of the power of vowels – Faaala.

On my return to Savai'i I found that nothing to do with the refurbishment was true. Nothing had been done and there were no plans to do anything. I did, however, meet Seilala, and he was very welcoming. He and his wife, Luti, were to become dear friends, and the two weeks we spent in their large *fale* were the best introduction I could have had to my new life. Seilala counselled me not to be angry with Maiava. 'He wanted you to be happy, to stop worrying,' he said. 'If he had told the truth you would have been sad and there was no point in that. You must relax and wait for the work to be done.'

The first day of school left me stunned. The students — girls in blue skirts and white blouses, boys in white shirts and blue lavalava — lined up for assembly in lines that surpassed anything the King's College battalion could have achieved. They sang hymns, and the Lord's Prayer, in a soft harmony that would have stopped Mr L C M Saunders in mid-stride. Teachers shouted at them.

I took a walk around the classrooms, firstly from the outside, peering through the wire netting and more or less hidden in the bushes. Then I went boldly inside, viewing the work of my teachers, many of them older than me. They were violent. They hit children with their heavy hands, with sticks and *salu*, a short broom made from the stinging and nasty ribs of coconut leaves. I witnessed one teacher instruct others to thump one of their fellows. Steve used to get his dogs to turn on a misbehaving brother, which they did with noise and enthusiasm. This classroom attack was worse.

I suppose I believe the occasional wallop with an open hand might not be out of place — to restrain, to stop a fight, to curb impatience — but this systematic use of force horrified me. I went back to my office, a stuffy little room under a two-storeyed classroom, and stared at the wall. Slowly, the wall relinquished its wisdom — they were trying to show me what good teachers they were, fully aware of their responsibilities and the God-given task of teachers to rid their pupils of sin.

I called a staff meeting for after school, and gave an impassioned speech about corporal punishment. I issued an edict: 'Teachers are not to take sticks into the classroom!'

This was greeted with silence. As the staff filed out, Lemalu, who was about thirty years older than me, said, 'Thank you, Sir, for your fatherly advice.'

He was not being sarcastic.

The next day I went around the school again, lurking in the bushes like a good chicken farmer. All was calm, and teaching — that is, a teacher at the front, talking — seemed to be happening. However, one teacher, Aso, a strong young man at the beginning of a career as a professional boxer, was wielding a thin whistling stick in the traditional manner. I confronted him.

'You said no sticks,' he smiled. 'This is only a wire!'

We were referred to in the village as 'The family of teachers'. I had joined this family in the worst possible way, issuing edicts, taking away a main source of confidence by trying to ban corporal punishment. I had trampled on tradition and possibly on religious belief. It was going to be a long way back.

The first part of this journey was to rid myself of the ideas and ideals I had developed in the New Zealand education system, with its luxury of being able to stipulate 'free, secular and compulsory'. None of those things prevailed here. Families paid a significant percentage of their meagre income for their children to go to school, and this sacrifice was loaded with expectation. Religion pervaded all aspects of the school day, from the morning assembly to the perceived need for punishment. Attendance was not compulsory – children were either at school or working in the family gardens.

PALAULI JUNIOR HIGH SCHOOL had pupils from Forms One to Four. Those in Form One had won the right to be there by succeeding in exams at the end of Standard Four. For the 50 per cent of their peers who did not pass the exam, this was the end of their formal education. They would enter the village workforce with the stigma of educational failure added to the burdens they would carry every day. Our pupils in Form One and Two were faced with the nationwide exam at the end of their Form Two year. This exam would cut their numbers by a further 50 per cent.

These students were totally and exclusively committed to the dreaded exam. Nothing else counted. Art and folk dancing had no relevance here. The teachers' views and words were the holy grail to be committed to memory as fast as possible, ready to regurgitate at exam time.

I took a class outside and pointed at the sun.

'What is that?' I asked.

'The sun,' they chanted.

'No,' I said. 'It is the moon. The moon. Now, what is it?'

'The moon,' they chanted. 'The moon.'

They did not seem resentful or confused. They were a million years away from yelling 'Don't give us that bullshit, Teacher, that is the sun and we have always known it to be the sun.'

Back inside I tried to talk to them about scepticism, about asking questions and about being confident about what they knew. I tried to be silly, jokey and friendly. They sat patiently, ready to learn, wanting to learn, wanting me to give them what they needed for the exam.

Siainiu and I talked for hours and hours. She, as much as I, wanted to deliver a teaching programme that explored more than the exams: she, more than I, knew that we didn't have the luxury of doing this. We both lamented that for the children who failed the exam, what we were teaching them had little to no relevance to the realities of their lives.

This was especially true of the students in our Third and Fourth Form classes. They had won places here, but this school was not high on their list. If the universal hope was to get to Sāmoa College in Apia, then two years at Palauli Junior High School was unlikely to help them. They wanted to get government jobs, to become doctors and lawyers, teachers even. They wanted clean white shirts and long fingernails.

All the teachers at Palauli had let the nail on the little finger of their left hand grow long, sometimes long enough to curl. This was the outward and visible sign of not doing any manual labour. By the end of my first year there, I had involved them in sufficient gardening, digging, sports, building and steady propaganda to have killed all the long nails, some of them painfully. The staff grinned and at times grimaced at me and called me a peasant. I was very proud.

The exam had to be paramount. In our first year in Palauli, I did my best to learn and accept this, but I did not do enough and the exam results were poor. Entry to Sāmoa College was, rightly or wrongly, the benchmark by which we were to be measured. One student, a clever girl who would have triumphed wherever she was, achieved this, and about half of the other students gained entry to various schools, ours included. For the remaining fifty or so students, that was it. Their life was to be in the village, white-collar dreams extinguished, the heavy financial investment their families had made producing no reward.

As I saw it, life in a rural Sāmoan village was hard. People got up early and walked up to eight kilometres to their plantation. The work was heavy and sweaty. At about eleven o'clock they would eat, and rest for a while, before harvesting all they could carry, filling great baskets that swung from the end of a pole that was heaved onto the shoulder. They then set off on the long journey home. Most walked with a rhythmical bouncing step that eased the burden and perhaps shortened the journey. These people, the village workers, both men and women, were lean and fit. They were strong and muscular, with feet turned to leather by the stones of the road.

It was easy, at Christmas time, to identify people who lived in New Zealand and had come back to spend time with family. In contrast to the local people – people to whom they were generous to the point of their own detriment – they had a sleekness about them. They weighed more, they had more, and they knew that however difficult their New Zealand job might have been, it was easier than the daily trip to the plantation. They had escaped the village and its hardships, but in the process they had lost the physical fitness of their village relatives.

Our village consisted of the three sub-villages, or *pitonu'u*, of Faaala, Vaito'omuli and Vailoa. They were grouped around a huge lagoon with a reef several kilometres from the shore. The shore was rocky, as in sharp volcanic rocky. At every fifty metres or so were the euphemistically named *fale ʻuila* or bicycle sheds. These were toilets balanced at the end of precarious, rickety jetties. The belief that the tide would flush away the sewage of the village was ill-founded, and the shoreline was polluted, unpleasant and dangerous. People recognising it as a foul place dumped their rubbish there. This was no airline-poster tropical beach. And the tropical fish that so many people keep in carefully tended tanks and believe to be beautiful? All I can say is that they are indiscriminate eaters in their natural state, if third-world toilet arrangements can be called natural.

Sometimes we would walk several kilometres through the bush to an idyllic beach near the reef. It had its own small reef and the sort of sand I had expected to see everywhere. We would relax there, but would long for the endless beauty of the beaches and rock pools of Siainiu's home village, Safune.

When the first year's exam results were published, we were invited to a meeting of the *fono*, the gathering of matai. This gathering decided everything about the village, from education to water pipes. It was headed by a magnificent person called Momoisea. He was a judge, based in Apia but he would return to Vaitoʻomuli most weekends. He was a huge man both physically and spiritually, known throughout the village for his dispensing of wisdom and US dollars. (Here I must interrupt myself to say the US dollar was then worth 70 cents in New Zealand money. The Sāmoan dollar was $NZ1.20. Times have changed – the *tālā* is now worth about 58 cents!)

Momoisea presided over the fono the evening we were called to account for the exam results. He helped moderate people's expression of disappointment. He also dispensed orange cordial laced heavily with gin and the luxury of ice. This hospitality did not help at all. Basically, the people had expected Siainiu, as a scholarship student, and me, as a New Zealand teacher, to deliver miracles. I tried to muster a reply, made difficult by the need for one of the teachers to translate for me and by the increasing discomfort of sitting cross-legged. We stumbled on, and then Siainiu began speaking.

Her formal Sāmoan was immaculate, as was her knowledge of the historical and biblical references that are essential in Sāmoan oratory. Men who didn't usually listen to women listened to her. They listened because they recognised that the quality of her speech-making was higher than theirs. Basically, as far as I could understand, she told them to have patience, to be grateful we were here, and to wait a reasonable time before they expected miracles. I watched her sway the room.

I hate it when I hear European men who have married Pasifika or Māori women describe their wife as being a princess from a royal line, which somehow means they haven't stooped as low as they fear their friends and family might think. Siainiu was not high-born, but on this night she did become regal. As I watched and listened, through the sweetness of the cordial and the bite of the gin, I realised again how much I loved and admired her.

I also realised that the exam was the only thing that mattered. I would focus on it exclusively.

We left and steered each other across the *malae*, the village green, to our house, passing everyone in the village who had gathered to listen and watch. We were drunk and weeping with disappointment, but determined to get to the relative privacy of our house before throwing up, as we both desperately wanted to do.

8.

I HAD THE best and biggest vegetable garden I have ever had. No, I should not have said 'I': the whole family worked in it, and family meant a considerable number of people. Siainiu's parents spent a lot of time with us, and her young cousin Gaui was chief Lope-minder, a job she did with beauty and intuition. Sundry other cousins lived with us because they went to our school. Ema and Siaosi, two of the children of Siainiu's recently deceased brother, Sia, came to us after their mother abandoned them. It was a booming, pulsating household in which everyone contributed as best they could. It was a long way from my hut in Papuni.

We had electricity, thanks to a generator with an ancient Lister diesel motor that I fought to keep alive, even though its life was a noisy, polluting affair. It powered lights, my indispensable stereo and little else. It wasn't interested in anything that involved heat, so we cooked on a cantankerous kerosene stove, the big brother of a camping Primus. It looked like a conventional stove with an oven and four burners, but it needed extensive foreplay to get it to function. We once cooked a leg of mutton that we decided to believe had remained frozen for its entire journey from New Zealand. Unlike the legs of mutton I had buried in the dead of night, we treated this one as a gift from the gods. Thanks to the advice and constant observation of almost everyone in the house, the leg cooked beautifully. The slight taint of kerosene would have been drowned by mint sauce if we had had any, but that didn't curb appetites.

We hungered for protein and for fresh vegetables. We were people who greeted the arrival of mutton flaps at the Saleloga Morris Hedstrom Store as an occasion to celebrate. The garden helped, as did our special chicken house, but there were long periods of the blandest of diets — tinned herrings and taro, even *ta'amū*, taro's large, coarse cousin. We would wait for new season's breadfruit to be ready and grieve that our efforts to grow potatoes were a failure.

I had read a little book from Indonesia that gave advice on making your back yard productive. It became my bible, along with notions of hippie self-sufficiency. The chickens lived on a deep litter of sawdust we collected from a local sawmill. Every six months we shovelled this onto the garden, much to the delight of the plants. They grew with an enthusiasm that can only come with warmth and plentiful rain. Weeds had a greater enthusiasm, but were largely dealt to by my mother-in-law, Sasao. She would rise early and sit cross-legged in the garden, pulling weeds and singing hymns loudly enough to wake the household and drag reluctant sleepy children and teenagers to join her in both song and labour.

I could write so much more about this wonderful, independent, laughing, irreverent survivor of a woman. Perhaps it suffices to say here that whenever she left our house, especially after she had acquired a large suitcase, we had to stop her and do a bit of a search. She had strong Robin Hood sentiments, and would pack a number of our possessions, especially clothes, to distribute to her less-fortunate children and grandchildren. These searches would involve her and her daughter exchanging words that if I had uttered them to my parents would have caused ten years of silence. Siainiu and Sasao knew their relationship and love could not be mutated by words, and this gave them both a lot of freedom.

I would sometimes walk home across the malae from the school, listen to the teachers walk back to their houses singing a chorus from Handel's Messiah in gently exuberant harmony, dodge the young men playing rugby despite the rocky outcrops that littered the malae, and feel an all-encompassing contentment. Lope would run (toddle?) to meet me and we would, at her insistence, inspect the garden and talk to the chooks. I would go inside, chat to Siainiu, now pregnant with our second child, and drink a cold beer from our fridge, another shaky kerosene miracle.

My feelings of bliss would be interrupted by the village curfew bell calling us to evening prayer. I would sit through Siainiu's father, Matalavea, praying, singing, extolling, for at least half an hour, sometimes concentrating to follow the language, but usually going into a dreamy state as I mulled over plans for school, family and garden.

Of course, it wasn't all contentment. An array of creatures

found my thin skin and blood attractive. I had frequent infections from sores that would require yet another penicillin injection from the local Sāmoan doctor, known as an SMP (Sāmoan medical practitioner), a cheerful man who could make an injection feel like the kick of a mule. I also had to find time for my MA thesis, an ambitious work entitled 'The Diagnosis and Treatment of Disease in a Rural Samoan Village'. Thus far I had only thought up the title, but I was so pleased with it that I thought my supervisor, Tony Hooper, might grant me the degree based on it alone. We communicated by aerogramme, so the gap between ridiculous ambition and the dashing of that ambition was long enough for me to have arrived at the same conclusion.

Evening prayers could sometimes go on for longer than my dreaming could sustain. We went to church every Sunday – my belief was that the job demanded it. I marvelled at how the pastor's sense of our sin and evil drove him to new heights of anger and condemnation. People sat in areas of the church according to their status and village group: children, young untitled men, married women, unmarried women, and titled men. Siainiu and I sat together in our own special seat.

I would be horrified as I listened to the pastor read 'And Jesus said, suffer little children to come unto me' while the old chap with the long stick assigned to ensuring the children remained still and quiet acted as if he had heard only the word 'suffer.'

The plate would be passed around in a manner that suggested the process had been influenced by marketing advisers, with every donor and the size of their donation loudly announced. We put what we wanted to give in a brown envelope. At first, the collector would boom: 'Tim and Siainiu, honourable leaders of our school, one brown envelope.' As his disappointment grew over the weeks he changed this to 'small envelope' and then 'very small envelope'. In the end he would take the envelope and barely manage to mention our names.

9.

THIS WAS THE Year of the Exam. The teachers were delighted with this decision, glad to be freed from my fanciful ideas. They had felt threatened, at times, that I would take them away from the security of the things they had worked so hard to learn and to teach. They were proud of this knowledge. Soon after my arrival, they had asked me to confirm details of the rules of changing direct speech into reported speech, a matter that was given extraordinary importance in the English syllabus.

'When you change the imperfect tense into reported speech, you have to use the pluperfect tense. That's right, is it not?' asked Lemalu.

'I wouldn't have a bloody clue, mate, and I wouldn't know why you would want to do this.'

He was delighted with my reply. This was his area of expertise.

'Why do we teach this, Sir?' he replied. 'We teach it because it will be in the exam. The exam, Sir.'

I managed to stop him calling me 'Sir'; the revelation of my vast areas of ignorance probably helped him do this. I never really came to terms with the rules of direct and indirect speech, despite his repeated efforts to help.

The exam would involve a lot of reading, and it seemed important to give students as much practice as possible in reading exam papers. I made up and printed out on our faithful old Gestetner machine many mock exam papers. This involved hours turning its non-electric handle, trying to be slow and patient — it rejected and punished speed.

Here I must recount the visit of a UNESCO technological adviser to schools. On his first visit he proudly showed me the printing device he had invented. It involved a stencil, a bamboo frame, a small squeegee and a quite extraordinary amount of printing ink. He demonstrated this device in my office, where the ink, as well as his refusal to allow me to talk, left a lasting impression. When he did let me speak, I showed him the Gestetner in the adjacent storeroom. He left quite quickly, mumbling about my lack of gratitude.

I included tricks in my mock exams: 'In Section B only answer question one; in Section C all the answers are yes; write your name then draw an arrow through it. The arrow must travel right to left.' Our mantra was read the question, read the question, read the question. I had the impression that the students were starting to enjoy these exercises, to play 'where is Tim trying to be clever?'

Under the influence of Faanafi, the first indigenous Director of Education, the role of Sāmoan language and culture was given increased importance. Teachers allocated little time to this area on the grounds that Sāmoan was something they knew, and more time had to be given to the battle with

English. Siainiu and I saw this as not only a hugely important part of their learning but also an area where our students could excel, could gain marks. I asked Lemalu, the only matai on the staff, to be the specialist Sāmoan teacher. He relished the role, gave it status, and was more relieved than he cared to admit at leaving direct and indirect speech behind him.

Sua, the school inspector for Savai'i, would visit often. He was a serious man, nearing the end of his career. I found him helpful and reassuring. I also found I needed to find tactful ways around his need to give me advice, some of it sufficiently strong to merit being called instructions. He was at the school one morning when Faanafi made an unexpected visit. I greeted her, as one greets dear friends, with a hug and a kiss. After she left, Sua said, 'I will no longer come and give you instructions and advice.'

'Heavens,' I said. 'Whyever not? I look forward to your visits.'

'I saw that kiss,' he replied. 'You are free to do things your way.'

He did continue to come back, and we had many worthwhile discussions. Now that he felt free of the need to instruct, he became so much more valuable — became a friend, in a restrained kind of way.

In the middle of the year Faanafi asked us to organise a thank-you ceremony, known as a *ta'alolo*, for the United States Ambassador to New Zealand and the South Pacific. The ambassador, Kenneth Franzheim the Second, was referred to as the 'Arm-Pastor' by many of the students when they did the inevitable writing that followed such visits. He had organised the gifting of sets of out-of-date encyclopaedias to every school in Sāmoa. We enlisted the whole village and planned the ceremony. It would involve a parade of all the students and most of the village. In fact, the entire village, for who would stay home when there was an event of this magnitude to be witnessed? This would be followed by the formality of an 'ava ceremony. Later, there would be a feast.

The ambassador was brought to our house and we were to instruct him on procedures. It was unfortunate that his wife had decided to wear bright red 'hotpants', short, tight and more embedded in village memory than any of the many words said on that day. He asked what to do in the 'ava ceremony. I explained, then Siainiu explained more fully, that he would receive the cup first, as the high chief of the visiting party. He would raise it high, say the word *manuia* and then drink. He required many repetitions and we role-played the event, using my favourite dessert bowl as the cup. We warned him that he might have to sit cross-legged for several hours.

The parade through the village went well – our students, trained by Lemalu, performed beautifully. The matai, well aware of my struggles to sit cross-legged for any length of time, provided two chairs for the guests. Momoisea's wife tucked a lavalava around the hot pants and everyone relaxed. Perhaps lulled by the heat, or the long speeches, or whatever other concerns might have beset a Richard Nixon-appointed Republican oilman from Texas, the ambassador forgot his lines. He raised the cup and uttered 'Manure' in a loud voice. I said 'Jesus' in a voice louder than it should have been, and the village pastor looked at me, nodding his approval.

There was a gap before the feast would be ready, and

the ambassador's wife asked if she could use the bathroom. Fearing the potential disaster of negotiating her way to a fale 'uila over the lagoon, Siainiu suggested we go back to our house. After everyone had 'freshened up', we sat in our lounge talking. I had cranked up the generator and my little stereo was quietly playing Vivaldi's 'Four Seasons'. Actually, not all that quietly, thanks to the generator. Siainiu and Jorgina, a name Google has just returned me, were discussing the relative merits of sundry composers. Jorgina had a look that indicated this was not a discussion she thought she would have in this situation, with these people.

I had taken a few bottles of beer out of the fridge and placed them on the table, where they glistened with very inviting condensation. While I fussed around looking for a bottle opener, Siainiu, fully aware of what lay behind the expression of surprise, picked up each bottle, bit the tops off and spat them out of the corner of her mouth. She then smiled sweetly and continued to talk about Boccherini and Vivaldi. I said 'Jesus' again, but I don't think anyone noticed.

There are only two other things to say about this visit. Firstly, we received a thank-you letter several weeks later in which we were addressed as 'Dear Tim and Cianaciv'. Secondly, we never used the encyclopaedias.

All this raises the vexed question of aid to developing countries. We had two Peace Corps volunteers. The first, in 1970, was a lovely chap who made a worthwhile contribution. The second was less lovely — he seemed to think it was his duty to question everything from Sāmoan custom to the school finances. I was never sure why he felt entitled to do this. He was never sure why he had no friends. We also had several young women from New Zealand Volunteer Service Abroad (VSA).

Basically, all these people needed to be looked after and were, in fact, more of a burden than a help. I never came to terms with the assumption of their home countries that somehow one of their citizens, young, untrained and immature, could be a teacher in the host country. It can be justified only if you believe your nation is so superior that its school-leavers know enough to educate ignorant natives. In contrast, Australia sent a small number of volunteers, all mature adults and trained teachers, experts in their fields and entirely capable of looking after themselves. These well-paid and well-housed people ran teacher training courses that were well organised, challenging and significant. My brother-in-law Taimalie, accustomed to the help of 'experts', was fond of saying of them: ' "X" is an unknown quality and "spurt" is a drip under pressure.' He agreed that this did not apply to these excellent Australian teachers.

Similarly, I had offers from New Zealand service clubs to ship over old textbooks and discarded library books. They were disappointed when I refused their offers but invited them to send a small number of current books. There is little enough time for teaching without teaching out-of-date material.

The most dramatic event of that year was the killing of Momoisea's eldest son, a tall, handsome lad, home from studies at the University of the South Pacific in Apia. He was wandering the village late at night with a group of young men. A fight broke out and a machete was produced. He stepped between the combatants, aiming to stop the fight. In the process he received a fatal blow.

The next morning, we drove early to the wharf at Saleloga, knowing, correctly, that Momoisea would be on the first boat. We took him and his wife, Olive, back to the village. When we arrived, there were three matai from the killer's family sitting outside, their heads covered with fine mats in a ritual known as *ifoga*. They were supplicants, admitting the guilt of their family member and asking for forgiveness. The mats were gifts of great value, but they served to make their wearers sightless and vulnerable. If the apology was not accepted and the offended party believed in an eye for an eye and a tooth for a tooth, then they were totally vulnerable.

Olive leapt from our ute and raced towards the sitting figures, picking up and raising a rock as she ran. Momoisea, with speed I did not think such a big man could find, sped after her. He took the rock from her hand and, with his arm gently around her weeping figure, went to each of the supplicants and lifted the mat from his head. He offered his hand to help them off the ground. There would be punishment, imprisonment and retribution but there would be no more killing.

I watched in awe, tearful at the sight of such huge spirit and courage, overwhelmed that this society had established mechanisms to express remorse and forgiveness. I had come here to teach but there was so much to learn.

Momoisea died shortly after we returned to New Zealand, at the age of forty-nine. He left his wife, his eighteen children and a lasting impression on the many people he helped.

ON 7 AUGUST that year our son Peter was born. It was a long and difficult labour at the 'hospital' at the neighbouring village of Satupa'itea. Two village midwives were yelling at Siainiu to push. The SMP arrived. He had just completed a Diploma of Obstetrics in New Zealand and was working hard to raise the standards of midwifery. He had campaigned against yelling 'push' in every circumstance, so he turned on the vocal duo and, pointing to two small high windows, shouted, 'Why don't you find a strong ladder, climb up there and try to push your fat bodies through those windows and see how that feels!' They left in a huff, and the delivery seemed to go more easily after that.

I felt huge guilt about not having taken Siainiu to New Zealand for the birth – a guilt that was to turn into even larger feelings of regret. The problem was that we knew the whole experience could have been better. People can be happy with their lot until they hear or see a more attractive alternative. For example, the village would turn out to cut grass along the roadside and other public areas. They would swing their machetes in time to a series of songs. There would be jokes, laughter and a shared meal. This happy community time was shattered when someone was sent a motor mower from New Zealand. Mind you, the motor mower was borrowed by all and sundry and wore out after a few months. Then people picked up their machetes again, but the fun had gone out of it.

There is a Sāmoan concept called *gau*. This means impediment or fault, and it is reasoned that everyone has one or several of them. These may be obvious individual impediments, like a twisted leg, a blind eye or a harelip. If this is the case, the person is called by the name of the gau. Sione, a village man who attached himself to us as an invaluable odd-job man, had a permanent limp. He was known as Vae Pio, 'Crooked Leg'. If you had no obvious impediments, then you were ascribed the gau of the place where you were born. The gau of Satupa'itea was that the inhabitants ate stones. If this were true, they would have been well fed. Satupa'itea is surrounded by sea and covered with stones. We try not to remind Peter of this.

He was a happy, gurgly baby, perhaps because he was almost always being cradled by someone. Or it might have been the diet of stones. Matalavea usually sat beside the door. We would place Peter in his lap on our way to school and he would still be there when we came back. The old man sang to him, told him stories, and stroked him with hands hardened and bent by a lifetime of physical labour. Peter would be handed to a series of family members throughout the evening. He would then sleep with Siainiu, Lope and me in our bed. We had heard the warnings and organised four mattresses side by side on the floor. The wisdom of this was negated by the fact that inevitably we seemed to be crowded onto one of them by morning.

I kept working on my thesis, collecting the names of illnesses and exploring the ways in which they were grouped. This was under the umbrella of the then popular ethnoscience, which sought to investigate indigenous systems of labelling and classification. The most famous studies explored Inuit names and definitions for snow and other such questions. I searched in the boxes of index cards in the university library and found a lot of definitive material, including an article entitled: 'Is a Hamburger a Sandwich?' This question has plagued me ever since.

I was fascinated by the way many diseases in Sāmoa are ascribed to supernatural causes and ghosts, and spent hours listening to stories of conflicts with both 'national ghosts' known to everyone and the ghosts of dead relatives. I came back to New Zealand for a month to get more thesis guidance. After almost two years in the village, I was stunned by many things, but two in particular. The first was the amount of perfume people used. Waiting in a crowd for a pedestrian-crossing light to change, I'd find myself overwhelmed and have to move away. The second was the amount of butter people used. In our large household we ate a lot of bread made by the local baker in his big wood-fired ovens. Siainiu would organise a production line with the school-going cousins – one cut the bread, the next buttered it, and the last one in the line scrapped the butter off, leaving only the small residue that had melted into the bread.

My few weeks in Auckland were, perhaps, a mistake. I had needed reassurance about the direction of my thesis, and this came quickly. As people pointed out, I was in an ideal situation to collect data. All that needed to happen was for me to organise it properly. I think I knew this but had hoped to be given an easier answer.

Back in Savai'i I marvelled at how much both the garden and Peter had grown. It was a joy to be back – but there was much to do. The kerosene machinery had become grumpy while I was away and needed to be disciplined. The chip heater, which sat in a cupboard in the corner of the kitchen, needed to be cleaned out. It had a large appetite for firewood but was efficient at heating water. Unfortunately, it also heated the whole house, especially the kitchen.

Now I discovered it housed many large, heat-loving cockroaches, so I devised an elimination plan which involved me spraying the fetid darkness of the cupboard with fly spray. Four household members were to stand behind me, armed with rolled-up newspapers, ready to smash the cockroaches as they tried to escape. At first nothing happened, then a few cockroaches staggered out and were jubilantly despatched. What followed was mayhem. Hundreds if not thousands of the damned things poured out of the cupboard, covering the kitchen floor — a seething, speeding insect army. They ran over feet and up legs. My newspaper-wielding soldiers did their best but became overwhelmed and retreated. The household was not happy with me. The consensus was that I should have let sleeping bugs lie.

Cockroaches, garden, thesis and communicating with the cantankerous kerosene hearts and minds of the fridge and stove all had to put aside as final exam preparation became more and more frenzied. There were nerves, but we knew our kids were ready. Teachers had run extra classes on Saturday mornings, cramming in more information. It was, I know, dreadful teaching — aimed to pass exams, not to educate — but I sensed that our students were confident, that they would read the questions, and that if I told them the sun was the moon they would now laugh at me.

We knew that any students in Form Two who did not win a place in a school would have no further formal education. Somehow, in my first year the reality of this hadn't fully hit me. I think I had still seen the village as an idyllic place and thought staying there was a pleasant option. Now I had learned enough to know this wasn't the case. Village life was not nasty, brutish and short, but it was far from idyllic. I understood the need to get away.

Once the exams started, a strange calm fell upon us, on the school and the village. People told me it was all now in the hands of God. I suggested that some very influential, if lesser, beings were also involved, like those who set the questions and those who marked them.

The results came quickly. We announced them at a gathering of anxious parents and pupils. And they were a triumph. Every Form Two child gained entry to a school for the coming year. Eight were selected for Sāmoa College – an unprecedented number. Every parent danced, every child danced, and we teachers were made to dance with them. It was the only time I danced in Sāmoa with no consciousness of my lack of grace and rhythm. We had succeeded. The village and the Department of Education loved us. We would party, perhaps with Momoisea's orange and gin, definitely with the one dozen quart bottles of Steinlager I would buy. The teachers seldom drank, and the dozen was enough to put all eight of them on their ears.

I celebrated, gave and received congratulations, but kept returning to one thought – the hope that their next schools would be able to provide these children with something closer to a real education than we had managed to do.

10.

THE FOLLOWING YEAR, 1972, started so well.

The staff, including two new teachers, seemed confident and forward-looking. They had come to accept, outwardly at least, most of my ideas, including the strange one about not using sticks as an educational aid. The success of the last set of exams had given us heart. It had also raised village expectations to an impossibly high level. People from out of our area also wanted to come to Palauli Junior High School, because it was seen as giving automatic entry to Sāmoa College. The School Committee, which was the fono of matai wearing one of its many hats, suggested we could raise fees. I rejected this suggestion with so much more authority than I had had in previous years — success and the arrogance of youth are a dangerous combination.

My aim for the year was to address the needs of the Form Three and Four students, who were in their last two years of formal schooling. They were, in a way, a strange appendage in the school. There were only about thirty students at each level, and they did not have the challenge of an exam at the end of the year. This was it — they were destined to return to the village or, if good fortune smiled, to go to New Zealand. The material they were taught did not recognise this reality. The Sāmoan lessons were great. Some of the maths had some applicability, but the students' growing expertise with direct and indirect speech seemed unlikely to do them much good.

The syllabus I visualised involved health, nutrition, basic bookkeeping, and lots of horticulture and animal husbandry — a term that gave visiting experts from the Department of Agriculture a great deal of amusement. My own garden was thriving. We had sufficient vegetables to give plenty away. Our chickens and pigs were healthy and productive, even if the latter sensed some of my history and treated me warily.

The experts wanted to use our home garden as an example to show village people what could be done. I refused to let this happen. We had little money, but we had more than most and I had been able to spend some of it on wire netting, cement and buying chickens from the Agriculture Department's chicken-breeding programme. We had Black Orpingtons, Rhode Island Reds, White Leghorns, and various combinations of the above when my efforts to keep the breeds apart failed. These chickens were always going to be more productive than the tough scavengers that roamed the village. We also had a stone wall enclosing the garden. Occasionally, a village pig would breach this wall and chomp into my lettuces. When that happened, we tied the pigs up and held them hostage until their owners repaired our wall. Why they didn't tell us to get stuffed and just retrieve their animals I don't know.

I knew that a horticultural programme at the school would succeed only if we could fence off an area of the grounds. I had purchased pipe and netting for that purpose when I was back in New Zealand, and enlisted the help of the teachers in building it. But every night people from the village would pull down whatever we had done. I appealed to the fono, the same fono that had agreed to my use of school funds to buy and import the materials, and asked them to find the culprits. I was sure that everyone, except me, knew who was doing this and why, but it became clear it was all part of a polite but implacable resistance to my proposed curriculum changes. They wanted their children to learn improbable things about English grammar, to nurture the white-collar dream, and to shun my efforts to say: 'You are going to stay in the village. Let me try to teach you things that may make your life easier.'

After half a dozen efforts to build the fence, Siainiu and I resolved to leave the village at the end of the year. I was keen to become the principal of Avele Agricultural College in Apia, and discussed this with Faanafi both in her role as Director of Education and as a friend. We glossed over my lack of agricultural and horticultural qualifications. We had given her lettuces and sweetcorn every time she had visited – this seemed sufficient qualification. Neither of us brought up the fact that the school already had a principal. I left this question to her.

Our children were thriving. Lope was a clever, active little girl who spoke Sāmoan as her first language. She had the run of the village and trotted around charming everyone. It is said it takes a village to raise a child – it also takes a village to spoil a child. Peter, still a baby, became bonnier and bigger by the day. In my limited knowledge of Sāmoan language I did as most language beginners do and picked up the vocabulary of my areas of greatest interest. I grasped an array of words to do with child-raising: *faiaso* – to behave in a spoilt manner; *tagivale* – crybaby; *fa'asisila* – to try to obtain food from an adult's plate; *'aisi* – to beg for food.

Everyone would sleep on Sunday afternoons, their tummies full of food from the *to'ona'i*, Sunday's special meal, and their souls full of the pastor's rant. But Lope did not, would not, sleep, and she and I spent this slumber time walking around the village, her telling me long fanciful stories, me thinking how nice sleep would be.

There would be times when I would look at my family, the garden, the school and the prospect of running an agricultural college and be overwhelmed by my good fortune. I was an accidental teacher but so glad about the accident.

ONE SUNDAY NIGHT early in March 1972, Siainiu and I were in bed, enjoying the quiet of the house and talking softly about the coming week. My hand was running over the warm familiarity of her body when my fingers found the cold unfamiliarity of a lump. A hard, rough-edged little lump about the size and feel of a dried pea. It radiated an evil, electrical pulse. I turned away as a series of images flooded through my head: images of illness and surgery, pain and suffering. Images of death. Images presenting themselves as an unarguable truth that I would have to deny, that we would have to deny, if we were to defy the fears that started to consume us. We clung to each other and started to make plans, very different plans.

The next day we saw the SMP. He examined Siainiu and said, 'This is either cancer or TB. Either way you will die.' As I have mentioned, he specialised in kicking like a mule. We went home, telling each other he was stupid, very stupid. But we followed his recommendation that Siainiu go to Moto'otua Hospital in Apia and have a biopsy.

I remembered times in childhood running down hills. Some of them were steep, grassy hills that tricked my feet and legs into going much faster than I had intended. The speed was exhilarating, but I knew that if I tried to change direction, or stop, I would surely crash. There was a hill of sawdust at the sawmill in Kaikohe. I ran down it with giant strides, my feet going deeper and deeper. At the bottom there was a flat area that I knew would be a safe place when I arrived there. I did get there, but found it was a pond with sawdust floating on the surface. My safe place was a trap and I would likely have drowned if my mates hadn't helped me out.

For the weeks and months after the SMP had delivered his mule kick, life became a series of these hills. There was speed but not much control; safety was often a deception. We were glad the biopsy was quick to arrange, but devastated at the slowness of the results. After two weeks of waiting we found there was a dispute at the hospital – up until that point biopsies of this nature had been sent to New Zealand for analysis, but doctors in the pathology department felt they were competent to do this work. While they argued, undiagnosed material waited in a fridge somewhere, waited while vanity and ambition raged. Our only course of action was to pack up our little family, a few possessions, a lot of dreams, and flee to New Zealand.

In the course of the next two weeks I handed the reins of the school to Lemalu, who tearfully accepted them. The village knew we were leaving and there was sadness about this, but there was also a willingness to help us get rid of our excess possessions. The wire netting around our chooks, the chooks themselves, the pigs and garden were seen as treasure. I indicated I would give all this away but, before I could nominate who I would give it to, people came and removed everything. My precious little farm disappeared before my eyes. The weeds knew they would now hold dominion.

I was outraged, just as I had been outraged whenever we had a feast at school. There was an unspoken signal, at a decent interval after the speeches and eating, when it was deemed the function was over. Women would then scramble to fill the baskets they had brought with whatever food they could grab. Dignity and control went out the window in the push and shove. I raved to Siainiu about the hypocrisy and the lack of morality this action showed. She pointed out that when you live at a subsistence level, the primary morality was loyalty to your family, and if this meant snatching a piece of taro from a neighbour's hand or walking off with my prized Rhode Island Red rooster, then so be it.

After a week we were in Apia, staying with Vaifou, who knew better than to try to beat the original sin out of our children. We still had Siainiu's niece Ema with us, and knew we couldn't leave this fragile child behind. The previous year she'd had the experience of developing sores on her head, which resulted in all her hair being cut off so treatment could happen. As was the custom, she was now called Poʻupoʻua, which means 'covered with sores'. She endured this and slowly her hair grew back, but after a few months the sores returned. I stood with her as her head was shaved for a second time. She made no sound, but large tears flowed from her eyes, eyes which showed a spirit teetering on the edge of surrender.

The people in the New Zealand Consulate and the courts were sympathetic, but said it would not be possible to adopt a child and have her entered on a New Zealand passport within a week. We were in full-steam-downhill mode, and somehow we persuaded them to run with us and it was done.

I still have a photo of the many family and friends who came to Faleolo Airport to farewell us. It shows Siainiu and me, together with our three little children, marvelling that we were on solid ground, not drowned beneath some deceptive surface.

Auckland was cold. Strangely, my parents, with whom we had hoped to stay, were also cold. They had organised a rental house for us. It was cold, too, but none of this could be dwelt on. We needed to organise medical treatment for Siainiu and a job for me.

I went to the Auckland Education Board, then the controller of school employment and property. Mrs Walsh is remembered by me and others as the employment angel for relief teachers — those of us whose circumstances meant we were unable to apply for the stability of a permanent job. She placed me in a special-needs class not far from where we were living. I was grateful but I should never have pursued a teaching job. I should have gone back to truck driving, should have realised that my emotional state meant I had little to give in the classroom.

Hospital, mastectomy, pain, worry and gentle recovery. Siainiu's spirit was so strong. She taught the other women in her ward a Sāmoan *siva*, its graceful movements so much better for their arms and destroyed chests than the physiotherapist's 'one-two, one-two'. When she was ready to leave hospital I sought advice from the senior surgeon.

'There is no way of knowing what will happen,' he said. 'I advise you to live your lives with hope. To put aside fear and believe that you are going to win.'

This is what we wanted to hear. I applied for a secondary teaching job at Ruawai College on the kūmara flats about 150 kilometres from Auckland. This was a mistake, but we had no money, despite the great wad of American dollars Momoisea had given us when we left his village. At the time a US dollar was worth about seventy cents — we should have waited before we cashed them in. The great attraction of Ruawai was that a house went with the job.

I was to teach English, history and social studies. Except I don't think I taught a damned thing. For the first and thankfully the last time in my teaching career I could not control my classes. It was a humiliating experience to stand in front of class after class, powerless to quell the students' racket, to fend off their jibes, to begin to teach. One day I exploded in rage and ranted about how lucky they were, how they didn't have to sit a murderous exam, how they had every chance in the world. In my rage I found my voice becoming thin and shrill, and then silenced by tears that had been waiting too long to be acknowledged.

At home, Siainiu, proud, fashionable Siainiu, could not find the energy to get out of her night clothes, to do anything more than give the children small bursts of attention. We took time before we could face the reality of her sickness returning, of the foolish optimism of continuing to adhere to the surgeon's advice. I took a day off school and drove her to Auckland – to the hospital. This journey could be done in about two hours, but on this day it took five. Five hours, oblivious of the cars trying to honk us out of our dawdle, oblivious of the children's restlessness.

She died on 5 August 1972. Peter turned one on 7 August. Her family, the 'aiga, organised a funeral with a cast of hundreds. They knew I wasn't capable of doing this, just as they knew I wasn't really capable of bringing up my children. Siainiu was buried in the Māngere Lawn Cemetery. When the final prayer had been said, the final hymn sung, people turned and started to move away.

At this point, somewhere in her three-year-old heart and soul, Penelope understood her mother had gone, and with her mother her chances of being a truly bicultural, bilingual person. She began a wail that became a keening noise, ancient and raw, strong beyond her years, beyond my tears and understanding. Everyone was stopped in their tracks.

I gathered up my children and took them through the frozen crowd.

Took them and hid.

11.

IF I WERE to give titles to these chapters I would call this one 'The Bleak Years'. I don't remember how many there were. I was teaching at an intermediate school in South Auckland. My teaching was competent enough, in an empty, formulaic kind of way. Again, the highlights with my class revolved around physical activities. We developed a special way of playing long ball – a simple game in which there are two teams, one of fielders, one of runners. The runners have to try to get to the end of the designated field before the fielders can hit them with a tennis ball – bullrush, but you only get stung with a tennis ball, not crunched in a crash tackle. It involves running, throwing, chases, near-misses and heaps of excitement. The class loved the game and did not want me to dream up anything else. We would work, then race out to the field three or four times a day, much to the consternation of the principal. Fortunately, he conducted school-wide tests on a regular basis. My kids always did very well, partly because they got to run around, partly because test and exam passing was now my speciality.

Folk dancing again proved a hit. For a school concert we prepared a couple of spectacular-looking dances. After our final rehearsal the students, in a flush of about-to-be-teenagers enthusiasm, decided they would dress in jeans, checked shirts and bare feet, their notion of how the Wild West would have been. They danced with huge gusto, whirling, skipping, jumping, much to the audience's delight. The next day they all had blisters the size of a traditional fifty-cent piece on the bottom of their feet. There is a certain guilt that falls upon a teacher when he observes his class limping for days because of an activity he set up.

I had myself intact enough to teach, to get Lope and Peter minded. Ema had gone to live with her uncle Tauta — yet another difficult change for her. I put together a semblance of life, but it was a rocky road with many potholes and tricky corners. I would like to look back and say I handled all this with monastic stoicism, but I did not. I formed a relationship with Elizabeth, a teacher from the school. I had recurrent thoughts about how it would have been so much better for the children if Siainiu had survived and I had died. The last prayers I ever uttered were to this effect.

If I was seeking to be punished for surviving, then this relationship provided that in large measure. I believed that marriage was a happy estate, that all the things I knew to be shaky in my relationship with Elizabeth would come right if we were married. We did this almost secretly, and then took ourselves to the Hokianga and the excitement of the first year of Ōpononi Area School under the leadership of Mike Mulqueen, the most energetic, visionary and courageous principal I ever worked with. He, almost single-handed, hounded the contractors assembling the school from a combination of new buildings and ones salvaged from the closed Waiotemarama District High School. There was a special excitement as we, a new group of teachers, worked to make a school and to make our homes. Our houses, our lovely school houses, were planted on bare blocks of sand, and there was an expectation that we would develop grounds and gardens. I loved doing this. I hid from reality in my teaching and gardening, both of which blossomed.

I came to think that Elizabeth was a bad person who had tricked me into marriage and did not treat my children well. Now, of course, I realise that nobody could have lived up to my expectations, not all of them unconscious, that the life I once knew would be replicated. She couldn't cope – a saint wouldn't have been able to cope, and she wasn't one of those. She left at the end of our first year at Ōpononi.

I taught English, history and Māori language to the small Fifth Form classes. Our focus was getting through School Certificate – bloody exams again – and we largely succeeded. I think we also managed, for a while, to run a happy school, although we had risked this in the first few days. Most of us had come from tough schools in suburban Auckland and we brought our survival strategies with us. This meant we came down like the proverbial ton of bricks on anyone who put a foot even slightly out of line. Our small collection of peaceful rural kids must have thought we were mad.

I HAVE MANY teaching memories from Ōpononi, happy memories. A wonderful Fourth Form girl, Eva Dunn, responding to a social studies homework question that asked for a graph comparing the populations of New Zealand and China with a small New Zealand stick figure beside a huge Chinese foot. Camping with Fifth Formers across the harbour beside the sandhills, where we scavenged for food and a couple of boys brought back illicit, delicious toheroa which they dubbed 'albino mussels'. We took our first successful Fifth Formers to dinner at the Kaikohe Hotel one Saturday night. There was a band called The Aphrodisiacs, and Matilda, perhaps the most gentle and serene soul I ever taught, asked if Aphrodisiacs was like Afro haircuts. I broke my promise to myself that I would always tell the truth to pupils and said yes, they were the same.

A local farmer took me fishing one Saturday. If you are able to anchor safely at low tide at the Hokianga Harbour entrance, and there is an easterly wind to flatten the waves, the fishing is bountiful. We came back to shore with a load of fish that would have excited an inspector, had there been limits at the time. The farmer hitched up the boat to his ute and manoeuvred it with casual expertise up the rudimentary ramp, later backing it into a tight space beside his barn. I expressed admiration for his ability and said I wished I knew how to back a trailer. He said he would be happy to teach me, and grabbed his farm trailer and hitched it to the back of my car. He then snapped on a large padlock.

'There ya go,' he said. 'I'll unlock it in two weeks. You should know how to back it by then.'

We don't remember what we are taught, but we certainly remember *how* we were taught.

I wanted to stay, to have my children grow up here, to enjoy the teaching, the fishing and that sense of belonging and mutual knowledge that can come in a small rural community. But I couldn't stay. I stuffed it all up by falling in love with the wife of one of my colleagues.

I became besotted with her and she with me. We hurled ourselves into a wild, doomed, foolish romance. We soared to wonderful heights and crashed from them perhaps not as heavily as people thought we should. There was hurt and destruction for her as she returned to the husband she didn't love and the two children she did love, and for me as I packed up the small tatters of my life and headed for a Scale A job in Auckland. But the greatest hurt was, and still is, to the daughter who was born of this reckless love, a daughter I wasn't allowed to bring up, a daughter still lost.

I had become the deputy principal at Ōpononi and was eyeing up principal jobs at other area schools. None of this was to be — the wages of sin, as my ever-judgemental parents said, the wages of stupid sin.

I limped into teaching in the Auckland school, notions of a high-flying career destroyed. I found I could still teach, in a kind of a way, on a careful autopilot, avoiding mistakes, avoiding excitement. I had been placed in an open-plan classroom with three teachers. The guy in charge modelled the running of it on the tag-wrestling concept — one person 'taught' the ninety-odd kids until he or she became tired, and then the next person took over. It was dreadful and I did nothing about it. I can't remember the children and I am damned sure they can't remember me.

Who saves us at these times? For me it was my children, their care and welfare, the need to give them some stability and fun, this last often being last. It was also friends, among them Peter from teachers' college, who kept driving trucks to pick me and my gear up from my disasters. He was the laughing Uncle Peter who drove the children out of their minds with excitement when he played silly games with them. We would have our Friday-night fish and chips together, and then he would return two overexcited kids who wouldn't sleep for ages, their faces flushed with more joy than they'd had in weeks with me. How do you thank people for such gifts? And Ken, who inspired me to teach better and set such an example of fine teaching. He once said to me, quite casually, 'I never feel prepared unless I have at least fifty alternative activities at the ready.' These were the days when I prepared as I walked towards the classroom.

My friend from Huapai, Wes, had become principal of the two-teacher school at Waipipi, just out of Waiuku on the magical Awhitū Peninsula. He suggested I leave the city and move to Waiuku. With his encouragement I took the plunge, and accepted a position at View Road School in Waiuku township, grateful too that a school house came with the job. School houses were both a salvation and a trap, but cheap rent saved me financially. With interest rates hovering around 20 per cent, the possibility of buying a house didn't seem worth even dreaming about.

I looked forward to running a class, but it was, in fact, several years before I became a classroom teacher again. Wes had run into problems. His marriage was beset with huge difficulties and finally crashed. He retained two of his five children; his lovely, lovely wife Jocelyn kept the other three. Wes had been riddled with self-doubt and conflicting feelings about the rigid faith of his childhood. The end of the marriage he wanted but couldn't live in, and some of its attendant deceptions, increased his insecurity to the extent that he admitted himself to the Kingseat Mental Hospital. A brave move by a courageous and honest man. This left Waipipi School without a principal, and I was asked to do the job.

I probably would have been better off if I had joined Wes in Kingseat, but was delighted to spend two happy terms at his school. I took the Standard Two to Form Two class, and the other teacher, Maureen, looked after the younger children. It was a happy, relaxed arrangement. I liked being back with primary-aged children and that my group was made up of many age levels. Again, I was given the chance to see the advantages of multi-level teaching in a rural setting. Again, the seeds of experimenting with this structure in an urban setting settled deep in my brain.

This little school was in many ways idyllic, but it was afflicted by two major problems I had never experienced before or since. The first was the wasps, hordes of them, making time outside difficult and risky. Eventually, it was a problem that was dealt to by local farmers with an array of flame throwers, agricultural chemicals and quite unwarranted hilarity, but for a while it shaped the environment. The second was more sinister. A new family arrived in the district and enrolled two children, aged seven and ten. These children were unsmiling and self-contained. They looked a bit dusty and their clothes were sombre. The other children avoided them, just as they tried to avoid the wasps, but the pair had a way of locking people into giving them attention. I often observed them in deep conversation with another child, not playing, not laughing, just talking with what seemed like great seriousness, usually standing while the listener sat. Parents complained. Their children were having nightmares, not sleeping, and talking of the end of the world being nigh because of their evil and wrongdoing.

I spoke to the two new children about their conversations. The sister, older and the leader, looked at me with pale, dead, unblinking eyes. She seemed untroubled by my questions and worked on turning the tables, questioning me about the state of my soul and did I know what was coming unless I changed. The implacable sense of judgement about her words disconcerted me. I felt I was being hunted, that she and the supportive echoes from her younger brother would not stop until I had submitted to their words. They wanted me to submit, to confess and to accept punishment. They had a strange, relentless power. They projected a cold, unspoken message of 'whatever you try you can't change or hurt me'. I am reluctant to call any children evil, but these two had a power that would not have been out of place in a novel by Stephen King.

I spoke with the School Committee, which consisted of most of the parents, about what to do. They were not witch hunters and, like me, were at a bit of a loss. The problem was solved when the family moved away as suddenly as they had come, leaving nothing but unpaid rent, dirty dishes and some haunted young minds. I don't know what happened to them, but I do know that as I write I feel something of the chill they were able to project.

The pleasant sojourn at Waipipi ended after two terms. Sadness at leaving was much mitigated by the news of Wes finding himself strong enough to return.

View Road School, to which I'd initially been appointed, was a strange beast that ran from Standard Three to Form Two. It was allied with George Street School, over a kilometre away, with a principal who was supposed to treat them as one school. The reason for this structure had, as is so often the case, little to do with educational theory and much to do with economic expediency. Waiuku had been a quiet little rural town with a primary school and a high school. The town's population more than doubled with the establishment of the Glenbrook Steel Mill in 1968. The Hamilton Estate was built to house workers, many of them from the UK, in a collection of streets of organised blandness.

A new Waiuku College was rapidly built, and the primary school took over the old high school buildings. Nobody seemed to care that using the old high school site as a 'senior primary school' paid little regard to what was left behind at George Street — a school for children from five to eight. In my view, this did not work. The eight-year-olds, who were the top dogs, lacked the social maturity to handle such a role, and this gave the school an air of madness. It was equally mad to have the one principal trying to manage both sites. When I came back from Waipipi School, I intended to be a classroom teacher, but was asked to be acting deputy principal and charged with running the View Road site.

I don't think I was particularly qualified for this job, but people seemed overly impressed with the MA I had ground my way through in the turmoil after Siainiu died. She had sacrificed much so that I could study, and I felt driven to finish the degree as a tribute to her. In writing a thesis that attempted to outline Sāmoan beliefs about diseases, their classification and causes, I learned that many illnesses there are ascribed to supernatural causes. I feared Siainiu may have offended one of the *aitu* or ghosts that prowl the country – how else can you explain such a valuable person dying so young? The degree, with its not especially impressive Second Class Honours, Division One rating, seemed to make people think I could administer educational institutions. The link between social anthropology and school management eluded me, but I was happy that others believed it was there – administration is way less taxing than classroom teaching.

TIME IN WAIUKU allowed us to become better organised as a family. Lope and Peter grew physically and emotionally. We had a sense of our little unit standing not exactly against the world but capable of becoming a fortress if and when that became necessary. Sāmoan had been Lope's first and only language when we left Sāmoa. It was one of the lost treasures I think she had lamented in her profound wailing at her mother's funeral. But she very quickly became fluent in English, and both she and her brother did well at school, surviving the teachers who had them draw pictures of their family at the beginning of each year, create Mother's Day cards, and cope, along with many others, with knowing they lived outside the norm.

Peter was slow to learn to read. His teachers, good people that they were, wanted to give him extra help, take him out of the classroom and thus have him branded with the label of not quite making the grade. I knew he would learn to read when he was ready – perhaps all in a rush as I had. Why did I believe he would become a reader? There were four main reasons: he spoke well and could tell a story; he loved stories being read to him and would listen for as long as I had the energy to read; he could concentrate on a task of his choice for considerable periods of time; and he seemed physically strong and intact, with eyes and ears that served him well. We needed to wait.

I adopted this approach of waiting and not intervening in all the schools I worked in. I heard a teacher years later refer to it as my 'Little Bo Peep' theory of reading. (I am not going to explain why, here, but will leave you, Dear Reader, to work it out just as kids slow out of the reading blocks also work things out, given time.)

Peter became an excellent and enthusiastic reader. I can't emphasise the word 'enthusiastic' enough. As a teenager he carried *The Lord of the Rings* with him everywhere, tattered, read and re-read. As an adult he recommends books to me. In many ways, I am more concerned with the reading habits and attitudes people have when they are twenty-six, not when they are six. I try not to be repetitive, but I will say again, and probably again, that it is so important to wait until a child is ready for whatever it is you want them to learn. This does not mean you leave the pot plant neglected in the corner until it blooms or dies. Nor do you let it grow wild, spreading its unruliness over the walls and windows. It means you water it, nurture it, give it what you believe might help it grow, help it feel good about itself and wait until it decides, of its own accord, that it is time to flower. Of course, this doesn't work every time for everyone, but it does stop the millstones and albatrosses that weigh down the hearts and minds of those many, mainly boys, who arrive at reading a little bit later than the nimble-minded girls who, some of their parents might claim, learned to read prenatally. We need time, us boys, but that doesn't mean we won't get there.

I don't think I contributed much to View Road School, but it did hang together and lurch along. Many of the teachers, as is the way in small towns, had been there for a long time. They were not about to let the bearded, long-haired, bead- and embroidered-shirt-wearing pseudo-hippie that I had become alter their thinking and long-established practice.

One of these people was Cicely Tipler, a feisty woman with definite ideas of what should be — ideas she had successfully communicated to several generations of Waiuku children. It was seen as a privilege to be in her class. Parents knew that a year with her would ensure their children would have good manners and clean fingernails for the rest of their lives. Cicely and her husband, John, befriended us and became the nearest thing to grandparents my children ever experienced. John taught English at Waiuku College, where he was feared by all and sundry, perhaps not without reason. I did hear him say, on more than one occasion, that all disciplinary problems in New Zealand schools would be resolved if every teacher was granted one hanging each year. For my children, however, he had nothing but gentle kindness and conversations that expanded their minds.

Lope and Peter would stay with him and Cicely when I had weekends away, seeking the company of other long-haired bead-wearers, especially those with muslin dresses and flowers in their hair. In my first summer in Waiuku, Cicely and John took the children to their bach in Matapouri. The plan was for them to stay for three weeks. I looked upon this as a gift from the gods and planned to relish every moment of my freedom. In reality, I became lonely, and after a week I drove to Matapouri to join them. I suspect no one was all that pleased to see me.

WES AND I spent a lot of time together, swapping recipes and discussing the merits of various soap powders. We also rotary-hoed a significant portion of the Waipipi School grounds and grew a very large garden together. Our main crops were potatoes and kūmara, which we sold by the sackful. Our customers, most of them already friends, loved our produce and expressed the hope that neither of us would enter a successful relationship and have our energy diverted from the fields. Wes left Waipipi and joined the staff at View Road, which, thankfully, gave us a legitimate excuse to give up the gardening. It was good to be teaching with him again, to have an ally on the staff prepared to listen to and support new ideas.

A significant number of children at View Road School identified as Māori, but the school did not acknowledge their particular cultural and educational needs. They were to be assimilated as fast as possible, as recommended by Mr Hunn. I set up after-school te reo Māori lessons for staff. They were not well attended. I set up a three-day in-service course with the Māori advisers from the Ministry of Education. This did not go well — teachers were resistant, and the tutors locked into repeating what they had said a thousand times before. I despaired, seeing the fire I had tried to light becoming barely smoking embers.

These embers were blown into a brighter flame by our next guest, a local resident and mother, who came and spoke to the staff one evening. Her words were delivered with quiet dignity. She outlined injustice and the day-to-day struggle of being Māori in Waiuku in 1975. She spoke of how schools were so often foreign places for Māori children. She spoke of how many local Māori felt on the fringe of the King Movement, destined to serve but not to hold office. We listened and we changed a bit.

George Street and View Road were separated into two schools, each with a new principal. I ran around for a while, waving my plans for the future of the school, but couldn't find even a deaf ear on which to let them fall. I was tucked away back in a classroom, relieved yet resentful. The following year I was asked to organise a district-wide special-education venture that had just been funded. The idea was that schools would identify students who needed extra input, I would then select the neediest, and they would come to me for special training.

I was reluctant because I didn't think the model was either right or potentially successful. I was a supporter of what was then called mainstreaming, the inclusion of the child with additional needs in a classroom with their peers. Kids learn if they can be immersed in the same river as everyone else. They may not swim well, but the current and the help of those around them will let them travel further than if they are left safely on the riverbank, isolated and different. This belief was to play a significant role in my later teaching.

There was, however, some success. Parents from outlying schools drove into Waiuku so their children could spend time with me. I don't know if this time helped much, but I suspect the time in the car with their parents did. As parents we give such little one-to-one time to our children.

I remember one boy, small for his years, not able to read and a bit fearful of the world. I asked him what he most wanted to learn. He said that he wanted to be able to kick a rugby ball over the goal post. We worked on this every day. He wasn't especially well coordinated or strong, but we managed to get some technique established and he got the ball over more often than not. Admittedly, the ball had to be pretty close and right in front of the posts, but he could succeed, and success was something he had never previously enjoyed. Somehow, learning to read became easier, and everyone who thought I had been wasting time heaved a sigh of relief. Sadly, many believed he would have arrived at reading more quickly if I hadn't stuffed around with the rugby ball.

My four years in Waiuku did allow for lots of healing. I was still very conscious of the losses caused by both death and my own foolishness. There were times when this became overwhelming. At these times, I would leave the children with friends, pack food and sleeping bag, and go to the nearby long and wind-caressed Kariotahi Beach. Caressed wasn't always the right word – the wind could fall into rage without warning. I would walk as far as I could, then slip into my sleeping bag amid the sandhills, staring at stars, encompassed by the roar of the surf but still able to hear the remarkable multitude of creatures that scuttled through the windblown foliage around me. I didn't really think about anything specific at these times, didn't solve any special problems, but when I walked back along the beach in the morning, limbs a bit stiff and body in need of a cup of tea, I would feel lighter, resolved, ready to go back to my life and its troubles.

I spent time, in these years, with Linda, a young teacher full of ideas, music and beauty. She taught me some new ways of thinking about relationships, made me realise that I was, in so many ways, still locked into a traditional model of how men and women should behave. Siainiu and I had, without talking about it, fallen into traditional domestic roles and had the ease of similar expectations, even if some of those expectations could have been labelled sexist. Linda challenged me to see that most modern, thinking women would not want to live with a set of predefined roles. She was right but, man, it all confused the hell out of me. I found change hard, not being able to make all the assumptions I was so accustomed to making. She held up a mirror that I had not looked into for a long time, perhaps forever.

I also knew she was young and would need to move on, that when her two years at Waiuku were over she would be gone.

This was a sadness but also a relief — nothing would have been more fearful to me than having to make a commitment. Linda remains a very dear friend. I marvel at her journey from classroom teacher with music in her heart to lectureship at Auckland University, spreading the word about how music and music performance can be, and should be, a part of every child's life. A teacher after my own heart — interpret that as you will.

12.

THE TIME CAME to leave Waiuku and to try to kick-start my career. I won a job at Auckland's Mount Albert Primary as deputy principal, having slithered a bit further up the multi-coloured grading ladder. It was a scary move. I did not know where we would live, and I worried about schools for the children. Lope was ready for intermediate school and, believing as I did that intermediate schools were the product of a demented and expedient system, it was going to be hard to find anything vaguely suitable.

We ended up, through the accident of people we knew, renting an almost derelict house in magical Cheltenham Beach, the beach where Siainiu and I had lived so many lifetimes before. I scrubbed and improvised, and the house became more than okay. It was imbued, like an old classroom, with a quality I can only call liveability. A house to relax in and enjoy, even if the kitchen was inadequate, the water pipes clogged and the roof a bit casual about watertightness. The landlord intended to have it demolished at the end of the year, and said we could do whatever we liked with it.

The principal of Mount Albert Primary had been there for almost twenty years. He was an urbane and articulate man who seemed to believe that his mere presence was educationally beneficial. This belief exempted him both from doing any real work and from actually being there most of the time. He had done work in the past that had gained the enthusiasm of inspectors, who had showered him with the multi-coloured numbers. We clashed from Day One, when, as we walked up the stairs to meet with the teachers and plan the year, he said, 'Well, what shall we talk to them about? I think I'll tell them some of the history of this place and of the things I have done.'

I wanted class lists, distribution of resources, planning of sports days, setting goals, scheduling staff-meeting topics, play-ground duty rosters and an outline of planning requirements. I sat and listened to sixty minutes of history and fizzed. I resolved that it was my task to get him to shape up, to deliver the goods and not just talk about goods delivered in previous years.

I found that there was one classroom made up almost entirely of Pākehā children. It was taught by the most energetic and gifted teacher in the school. I saw this as a form of segregation and challenged the principal about it. He explained that the class had not been formed along racial or cultural lines. It was a class for families who were permanently settled in the area and unlikely to move away. Families of any race could prove themselves 'permanent', although it might take some time to do so.

Things came to a head when a parent–teacher interview evening was planned. The principal told me I was capable of running it and therefore he did not need to be there. In telling me this he included compliments about my ability, our teamwork, and how he was glad to be giving me the guidance and opportunity that only he could give. It surprised him that I was not grateful. I told him he had to be there, had to support his teachers, had to be ready to field any difficulties that might arise. He came, sat in his office with coffee and a book, smiling and avuncular. Halfway through the evening a serious problem did arise, and I took a rightly aggrieved parent to see him. The principal had gone, leaving a dirty cup and the aroma of expensive aftershave. The parent was not impressed with this, and not satisfied with the tentative compromise that was all I felt empowered to suggest.

It is true that when I let fly at him the next morning I drew on both my justified annoyance at his absence and the pool of long-held, unresolved frustrations. The fact that he hadn't arrived until shortly after 10 a.m. didn't help. I was in a full blast of red-faced rage, words I had prepared and ones that I never should have said pouring out of my mouth. I felt like a jet aircraft roaring at the end of the runway just about to explode into full take-off mode.

As my noise reached a crescendo, he raised his hands in supplication and said, 'Tim, Tim, when you attack me like this, I gain a greater understanding of how Jesus must have felt when the nails went through his hands and feet.'

I stopped. I had so many more words to say, but none of them volunteered to come forward.

Two weeks later he went on six months' extended sick leave and I was made acting principal. At the end of the year, after a few brief appearances, he resigned and used his grading to get promoted to a larger school. He told everyone I was the best deputy principal he had ever worked with.

MY FIRST IMPRESSION of the school was that it seemed almost out of control. There had been an influx of Pacific Island pupils and little had been done to meet their needs. The older boys ruled the playground. I made it my mission to curb their power and channel them towards positive activities. I spoke enough Sāmoan to reprimand them in a way that reminded them of home, even if I was not able to follow up with the familiar sticks and jandals. I visited homes to discuss behaviour, something that struck terror in the hearts of my playground pirates and bandits.

There were a number of confrontations. I recall challenging a ringleader, who became upset and accused me of picking on him, which was exactly what I was doing. Eventually, he fired his last shot over his shoulder as he ran from the school: 'I'm going to get my mother and she is going to come and beat your fuckin' soft head in!' I did meet her later and, yes, she seemed well capable of carrying out his threat. Fortunately, she liked me. I don't think he ever liked me, but he listened from then on.

After I had been at the school for a few weeks, I discovered that it had a school house at the back of the grounds. The journey from Cheltenham had become a frustration, all the more so because I needed to drop Lope off at Ponsonby Intermediate. My old mate Peter was working there and he would, I knew, look after her with avuncular enthusiasm. His new partner, Sue, was also at the school. She did so much to guide Lope through the mysteries of female growth, mysteries well beyond my ability to explain and certainly deserving more than my stumbling descriptions of plumbing. My gratitude to these two wonderful people will endure forever.

There was a teacher living in the school house, a single man some years older than me. I pulled rank, cited greater family need, and had him evicted so I could move in. He left the school shortly afterwards and disappeared into the country. Many of the staff actively disliked the fact that I had been instrumental in his departure.

I added to this dislike by becoming fanatical about playground duty. It is not easy for teachers to have to grab a quick cup of tea at morning interval or lunchtime and then have to patrol the playground, rather sitting in the staffroom, smoking cigarettes and gossiping about who has the worst child in their class. But if a playground is to be healthy and happy, free of both the casual and the systematic bullying that can occur anywhere, then there have to be adults around to be seen, to see, to hear and to counsel. Better still, there have to be adults ready to take part in games, to spot the lonely ones and walk with them, to tend injuries to body and spirit. In the best of playgrounds there are many activities and challenges, shade and sunshine, places to be quiet and places to be noisy. Increasingly, I found the staffroom uncomfortable. I had no desire to hear the complaints about children — why teach if you don't like children, I often wondered and sometimes found the courage to ask. In the playground I could have fun, keep my bowling arm in shape, and be there to help with the catastrophic griefs that hit children when they are excluded, when they aren't in the team, when their best friend has found a new best friend who walks around in triumph, firing shots on the betrayer's behalf. I also found it so worthwhile to sit or stand in a place where I could be invisible so that I could see and learn about what really happens.

A new principal was appointed at the end of my first year at the school. Much to my surprise and delight, it was my old friend Pius. I looked forward to working with him again and was sure we would make a happy, positive little team. Sadly, things were different. He was a changed man. His idealism and vision were still there, but they had become overlaid with caution and disappointment. He had had two serious car crashes and was coping with considerable pain throughout the day. The combination of pain and disillusion caused him to drink.

He, the man who had made sure I had everything I needed for some mad art projects at Beresford Street School, now berated his secretary for affixing stamps to letters in a way that did not meet his ideas of straightness and accuracy. As his anxiety increased, he would get to work earlier and earlier. We had a routine meeting every morning at 7.30, which was quite a challenge when I had kids to get off to school. Increasingly, he would express frustration about my lateness: 'I have been here for three hours and there are things I needed to talk with you about!'

I felt judgemental about both Pius and the former principal, without fully realising that much of what they did, or didn't do, was a reflection of the toll of the years. This was something I was destined to understand better.

RUGBY HAD A HUGE, perhaps unduly huge, influence on my time at Mount Albert. In my first year I took a hastily assembled team to play against a neighbouring school. We were soundly beaten and the players were crestfallen. Over the next four years I worked with them and other teams, and eventually we ended up beating everyone we played. Even if I say it myself, we (they?) played quite high-quality rugby. I ran lots of practices and there was rivalry to get into the team. It was unashamedly elitist – I wanted the best team possible, wanted the boys involved to feel they were the best in the district. They all knew that if they misbehaved they would be out of the team. I don't think I would do the same thing today, but I was proud of what we put together and pleased that this sporting outlet had a positive influence on playground behaviour.

I also recognised that I was alone in promoting sport and physical fitness at the school. Most of the other staff members were women, and they were open in expressing their lack of interest in these activities. I am heartened to see that today many female teachers are fabulously fit and keen advocates of children's sports.

The other rugby influence, in 1981, was the Springbok Tour. I was vehemently opposed to it and to the injustices of apartheid – I knew about Nelson Mandela, I had read *Cry, the Beloved Country*, I knew I could not go to South Africa with my children. I went on the first protest march in Auckland, and joined every other one except the very last. There were marches on Saturdays and Wednesdays. To sustain the energy to keep doing this I found myself simplifying my thinking – police were bad, the rugby union was bad, Ces Blazey and

Ron Don were especially bad, and Prime Minister Robert Muldoon was the worst pig of all. I condemned my pro-Tour friends and the apathetic people I worked with.

On one march the police tried to stop us entering the grounds of Kōwhai Intermediate School. I joined others tearing down one of the school's fences. It was about two metres high, made of pipe and heavy wire netting – a valuable fence that was part of the way the school kept its pupils safe – but we climbed it and forced it to fold to ground level. I, the deputy principal of the neighbouring school, cheered as loudly as anyone at its destruction.

If nothing else, I gained a sense of how easy it was to be swept along by a crowd. I also learned of the dangers of being in a crowd. I had resolved to keep myself safe by staying in the centre of the group. Not for me the front line – I had children to look after. However, the safe and noisy middle so easily and unexpectedly became the front, the side or the rear, exposed to irate rugby supporters and young baton-wielding police officers yelling, 'Stop or you will be hurt!' I had been taught that the police would tell you the time, help you when you were lost and stop bad people taking your things. I remain shocked that they wanted to hurt me and would risk hurting me seriously.

The Mount Albert school house was close to Eden Park, the target of many protests, and it became somewhere for people to come when marches finished. We would sit around, drinking and talking, then listen as each new group arrived, flushed, excited, all with a new story to tell of bad police behaviour, narrow escapes, injuries and things that had made them laugh. We had some great parties.

I had by then managed to buy my own house. Some friends had previously bought it so they could renovate it in partnership with one of their fathers. The partnership had dissolved into acrimony and all they wanted to do was get rid of the place. I hadn't gathered together much money and I dithered about what to do. I felt keenly the lack of a partner to talk with about it, to embolden me by saying: 'Let's do it!' Fortunately, my friends were patient and I finally got enough cash and gumption together to buy it.

I look back at all this as a moment as dangerous as any in my life. I had been in great danger of missing out on home ownership forever. I had a second mortgage at 19.5 per cent interest. This felt like a source of shame and I kept it secret. The cost of the house was $18,000, a figure that makes young people today collapse in weeping heaps. What was significant, as I am wont to tell anyone who will listen, is that I was paid, at the time, $8,500 per annum. I lament, as we all must lament, that you can no longer buy a house for twice a teacher's annual wage.

My jubilation at buying the house was dampened by my children. They were compliant, helpful, supportive, loving creatures who always filled me with enormous pride, but they refused to live in the new house. Every time we went near it, there would be weeping and wailing and gnashing of teeth. They would sit in the car and not come inside. They spoke of ghosts and evil spirits, and finally put me off. We stayed on in the house at the school. About a year later, I sold the property at a huge, unwarranted profit and purchased a house in Kingsland. I think this was the suburb the kids had always wanted to be in, and all their reaction to my first effort was just a lot of manipulative bullshit, something they deny to this day.

This second purchase was made possible by the profit made on the oh-so-lucky purchase of the first house. I had long quoted the words of John McKenzie, a Scottish socialist who became Minister of Lands in the Liberal government between 1891 and 1900. He, quoting John Stuart Mill, often said he didn't want New Zealand to become a land of the 'unearned increment'. I gained unearned increments from this house sale and was happy to have done so. The words we say when we are on the outside tend to be very different from the words we say when we are on the inside.

I also note that John McKenzie was a hero of mine in younger days. I applauded his desire for people to have equal access to land and not be ripped off by banks. I was saddened to discover recently that the land he happily distributed was largely obtained through tricky legislation he drafted so he could steal land from Māori, whom he regarded as inferior both as farmers and as God's creations. A fallen hero.

I think I became bored at Mount Albert Primary. I did not relish the role of being the go-between for the principal and the staff. Pius was increasingly stressed by the job, increasingly disappointed with small aspects of school life. We were all dedicated to the picking up of litter, as teachers the world over are, but Pius took this to new levels. He would bring samples of what he had picked up to school assemblies. The children started to think he had become the caretaker.

What had happened, of course, was that Pius had become burnt out. He had worked extraordinarily hard for many years and had done good things for a great number of children. I had seen him display remarkable courage when confronting a parent whose daughter had drawn a picture that strongly suggested sexual assault. The parent, and his wife, strongly, vehemently denied that any such thing was happening. Years later I read that his daughters, no longer silent, scared eight- and nine-year-olds, had formally laid charges, and the man was duly found guilty and incarcerated. Pius had chosen to do what he could, when many would have, and did, let such things pass as too dangerous and difficult. In the end, despite his bravery, he was powerless in the face of angry denial.

This sense of powerlessness when confronted by suspected physical and/or sexual abuse of the young children we work with is one of the great sadnesses of teaching. I remember Barry Crump writing in his book *A Good Keen Man* that he wished he had the power to peel back the bush so that he could see all the previously hidden deer standing there looking at him. Often when I saw large groups of children sitting quietly on the floor I would be overwhelmed. Statistics told me that some of them would be facing horrendous things at home. I wished I could peel back the bush and see what was really happening.

IN 1981, WHILE I was at Mount Albert, I wrote an article which was published in *Education*, a magazine the Department of Education produced and distributed to all schools. The article was entitled 'Meeting the Educational Needs of Maori Children'. It can be disconcerting reading material one published some forty years ago. I once heard a composer, in a radio interview, being asked how he felt about his early work. 'Ah, my early work,' he replied. 'All I can say is that I look upon it with affectionate contempt.'

I don't feel either of these things when I look at the article, but I do smile when I see what I think I was trying to say but hadn't formulated with the clarity that was to come later. What I was trying to say was that schools won't work for many children, particularly children from non-European backgrounds, unless we change the structure and values of our schools and get away from the educational model imported into the country by nineteenth-century British missionaries. There will be more, much more, about this later.

That year, too, I became involved with a new teacher on the staff. A good person, tall, elegant, conscientious and caring about her work. She was a runner who covered miles every day and a learner who studied every day. We spent eleven years together, nine of them married. It was all a huge mistake, a workplace attraction that should have been seen for what it was. My life of teaching and child-raising, especially now that the children were teenagers, was not for her. Her interest in pounding the pavements and going to restaurants was not for me, although I tried to pretend it was. Sometimes I would leave a restaurant and walk home by myself, my head full of pictures of my garden in Savai'i — she didn't have a chance, really.

We renovated the Kingsland house together, enduring weeks without a bathroom, labouring hard every weekend and trying to persuade ourselves this was the good life. She made it possible for me to do the travelling job I took up when I left Mount Albert, and for this I was deeply grateful. But when we finally parted it was with acrimony, regret and guilt. I behaved badly, but I had reached a point where I could no longer sustain all the life-support the marriage needed – the counselling, the drinking, the helpful friends, the reconciliations – and knew I had to pull the plug. I had dreaded being on my own, a weakness that had led me to plunge into this relationship, but now I relished the prospect of it being just me, interacting with Lope and Peter and their friends, rediscovering myself, being strong enough to be alone again.

This last paragraph has been the hardest to write. Up to this point I had lapsed into seeing myself if not as a kind of teacher hero, then at least as a caring, sensitive, sensible person. In this relationship I rediscovered my capacity for cruelty and unkindness – the person who had been capable of plunging a knife into a pig's heart was still there.

TOWARDS THE END of my fourth year at Mount Albert, my friend Peter rang me to talk about a job with the Correspondence School (TCS) he had seen advertised in the *Education Gazette*. This job was Auckland-based and involved travelling the region to visit students on the Correspondence School roll. I applied for it, and flew to Wellington to be interviewed.

This interview did not start well: the lift to the third-floor venue opened not into a passageway, as I had assumed, but directly into the interview room. As the doors opened, there were the interviewers in front of me. I was giving my trousers a final adjustment at the time, but managed to overcome my discombobulation sufficiently to launch into the interview and say enough to be offered the position. The fact that I had done both primary and secondary work was obviously in my favour.

I did a reality check with the person who rang to offer me the job. The more he talked about it, the more I wanted it, but it became clear it would involve at least one week a month away from home. For this reason, I declined — home was fraught enough as it was with arguments about hanging out washing and how many slices of bread had been eaten after school. My partner was training to become a school counsellor and was involved in many meetings at which people were invited to talk about themselves and their lives. She would introduce herself as the stepmother of two part-Sāmoan teenagers. She would tell me how sympathetic others were to this plight, and I would lose myself in a tailspin of resentment, sadness and powerlessness. I could not ask her to add 'absentee father' to this tale of woe.

The day after I declined the job I received a phone call from Jan Jackson. There were two Correspondence School 'regional representatives' (RRs) in Auckland. She was one and the position I had been offered was the other. Jan had been asked to talk to me about the job and see if she could persuade me to reconsider. After introducing herself, and being honest about her purpose, she said the most persuasive words possible: 'I am on Great Barrier Island, standing, in my gumboots, in the only phone box in Tryphena. The car I have hired has bald tyres and dodgy brakes, and I'm not sure if it will get me through the mud and rain to the guest house. I can't talk for long — I don't want darkness to be added to the challenge.'

I was hooked.

13.

THE JOB WITH TCS held many frustrations, but it also held many joys – I could teach, could use whatever teaching skills I had developed, but did not have to go to school. I could see pupils in their homes and find out so much more about them and their lives. When I joined, in 1984, the Correspondence School's romantic founding vision, set in 1922, could still be believed for a little longer: this was 'a school for the benefit of the most isolated children, for example lighthouse keepers and remote shepherds living upon small islands and mountainous districts'.

I was certainly a starter for small islands, mountainous districts and lighthouses and, to some extent, I experienced all of these, but the school's role as 'the school of last resort' was starting to be felt. It was getting harder to find genuinely remote children, and the school's roll was increasingly made up of those too unwell, or claiming to be too unwell, physically or psychologically, to attend day school; those who had been excluded from day school for behaviour deemed unacceptable;

those about to be excluded; pregnant schoolgirls; and an ill-defined group called 'itinerants'.

Many, if not most, families who enrolled had genuine reasons for doing so and a genuine desire to get their children back to school. Some, however, and quite a big 'some' at that, had manipulated the school's enrolment criteria and would have been better off facing up to the realities of going to their local schools on a daily basis. There were 'itinerants' living in buses that had grass growing higher than the wheels; sick children who ran up hills and down dales; people who said they knew they were faking it but who would, if so compelled, travel or go to a remote island if their enrolment was threatened. For many of these people, the Correspondence School represented freedom from 'the system', from the tyranny of school and school uniforms. For some, it was an extension of home schooling; for some it was a response to a set of religious beliefs; for some it was part of a convoluted world view which they were very happy to explain, in full, to anyone who visited; for others, the thought of someone coming near, especially someone with education on their mind, was fearful and repugnant.

As an RR I was not responsible for a pupil's programme and day-to-day teaching. This was the task of their Wellington-based teachers: a class teacher who handled pretty much everything at primary and pre-school level, and a form teacher who in conjunction with subject teachers provided programmes at secondary level. These teachers worked with great diligence in a building that never seemed ideal to me. Its three floors were crammed with small work areas — a desk, a chair, a bookshelf and an inevitable overflow of materials onto the floor. I found it hard to view these busy spaces without thinking of them as being populated by educational battery hens. It was a job I would have found very hard to do, but one that so many teachers did with admirable consistency. I'd have missed the daily face-to-face contact with students, the ups and downs, the conflicts to resolve, the growing up to be observed, and the sheer riotous fun that can be had with a group of kids who have found they can trust you.

The institution worked well, but only because of the good people who knew how to make it work, to organise and distribute the resources, to send them out, usually with personalised messages of encouragement. They would post hundreds of the famous green canvas bags of work, sadly soon to be replaced with less romantic green plastic ones. Without their commitment and routine, the whole organisation, teetering as it was on the edge of the computerised world, might have collapsed.

I would, on the week each term we had to spend in Wellington, gaze in wonder at the lurching complexity of it all. Two images repeatedly came to mind. The first was from the sundry black-and-white movies I had seen from upstairs in Kaikohe of rusty old cargo ships pounding through the cold Atlantic, pursued by U-boats and other evils. These ships would inevitably develop engine problems at vital stages, but there would be an engineer, usually called Scotty, who would know exactly which valve to turn, which bolt to tighten and which pipe to kick to get the damned thing to thunder back into life. TCS had such engineers. Their aim, of course, was to restore a busy hum rather than anything too thunderous, but it seemed certain that without their particular skills the school would have ground to a halt. The other image that haunted me came from words that I, rightly or wrongly, attribute to Karl Marx: 'The first people to shoot after the revolution are not the Conservatives, for we always knew where they stood. It is the Liberals, for they were the ones that made the unworkable systems continue to function.' I have not been able to find a reference for this quote and am starting to wonder, with egotistical optimism, if I made it up myself. Either way, it is true that only goodwill and dedication made TCS function at that stage. It was ripe for the huge shake-ups that occurred in the subsequent decades.

My task as an RR was to visit all the students on my roll — a vast collection of names that came and went, often before I was able to organise myself into contacting them. The role of an RR was to meet families and make their experience of working with TCS as smooth as possible. This involved a multitude of things. Ideally, we would be able to visit shortly after the first posting of materials arrived. If this was the case, we could sort out the confusing array of materials and give them an understandable order. Many, if not most, parents found the initial complexity of it all to be overwhelming and were daunted about making sense of the instructions. I have a belief that people confronted with something new and different need heaps of reassurance to get started. If the instruction says 'Now press Button B', most of us want to ask 'Does this mean I should press Button B now?'

Apart from this need for reassurance, many people did not, of course, give themselves long enough to come to terms with the task. I know that every time I have a kitset of some sort to assemble my first two reactions are:

1. The instructions are wrong, or poorly written, or deliberately confusing.
2. Vital components have been omitted.

If I give myself time, however, I usually manage to make sense of it all and discover the creators were not idiots after all. For the unsupported student with learning challenges, the mountain looked so big it was obviously not worth even starting to climb it.

An ideal first visit would involve heaps of reassurance, putting papers and booklets into manageable piles, setting short-term goals and checking that the levels of the materials sent were appropriate for the student. All this could be a positive and pleasant educational adventure. Everyone would be smiling and looking forward to getting started. This was particularly true of the students who had been excluded from school — although it must be said I didn't meet many of them. My letter giving the date and time of my visit was all too often a signal to the student to be somewhere else. But I had many wonderful conversations with those who did make themselves available, and who told me how glad they were to be away from their peers who had disrupted learning at school and mocked both their desire to learn and their educational shortcomings.

These new students, seated at the dining table in an empty house with an array of freshly sharpened pencils and a heart full of hope, would say things like: 'This is great, Tim, thanks, just what I want. I am gonna work hard. When will you come back?' I would have to tell them it would be at least six months before I could return. The light in their eyes would fade, the trust we had established would be shaken: they knew, I knew — everybody should have known — they wouldn't make it on their own.

I would sneak in a few extra visits, but these had to be hasty. I wrote furious letters outlining the need for more regular contact, and asking for my roll to be reduced from two hundred, with a high level of turnover, to something vaguely manageable, like fifty. Some number that would allow me to work properly, to make it worthwhile for a kid to invest faith in us and what we could offer. A sentence I used in all these letters was: 'If you plant a seed in a desert you have an ethical obligation to return and water it regularly.'

This image impressed me. It didn't impress anyone else.

At the time, there were ten of us doing this job. We were variously placed in Dunedin, Christchurch, Nelson, Wellington, Whanganui, Napier, Gisborne, Hamilton and, for two of us, Auckland. Each area was unique. In Christchurch and Dunedin the RR visited many long-established high-country farms where the tradition of TCS work was well established. Students would have their primary school years with TCS and then go to a private boarding school, usually the one their parents had attended. The majority of these folk were well organised in their practice and expectations. The RR had, and in fact had to have, a regular visiting schedule, with each family expecting to receive advice and compliments on their progress each term.

The chap in Nelson had a boat, many students in the Sounds and lots of adventures. Auckland was different. Jan, the wonderful Jan, covered the North Shore, North Auckland, and the smaller islands of the Hauraki Gulf, including Kawau and Rotoroa. I was allocated South Auckland, Great Barrier Island, some parts of the mid North, and one of the last remaining occupied lighthouses, Tiritiri Matangi. The majority of my students were in South Auckland and were on the roll because of some kind of problem. I found, when I started to understand the job a bit better, that it worked for me to immerse myself in the problem areas for three or four weeks and then fly to Great Barrier to balance myself up a bit.

My employment with TCS ended in 1987, but, very much to my surprise, I was to return to this work from 2001 to 2005, and again from 2009 to 2010. Both of these two unexpected bursts of employment showed that the main category of student enrolment was not isolation but problematical behaviours and backgrounds. This meant there had to be dramatic changes to the role of those of us involved in home visiting. These changes will be discussed when we get there, but for now I want to talk about the joys of 1984 when we could still imagine that we were educational gypsy minstrels, singing our educational songs in remote places.

Correspondence School work could be a wonderfully economic way of learning. Among rural families the mother − and it was nearly always the mother − had routines and expectations down to a fine art. Children would sit and work every morning and be largely free after lunch. It was a worry to me that the model was 'sit and work', but these tended to be children who had rural freedoms and tons of exercise. At primary school level, they would flourish if they had two major advantages. The first of these was a mother who had taken the time to learn and understand the systems, who was interested in her children's learning and able to present things as an adventure, not a chore. The second was a teacher in Wellington who was able to communicate, through letters and phone calls, a genuine understanding of the family, its learning styles and needs. I saw some deep and abiding friendships developed in this way, friendships in which teacher and parent were partners in a five-year-old learning to read (or a seven-year-old, if that was the case) and a Form Two student becoming confident with fractions and percentages.

For many, writing stories and letters became excellent skills. The successful student of TCS developed independent working habits and seemed to have conquered the pitfalls of procrastination. Most of all, they had at least two adults who had close, detailed and informed knowledge of their educational needs and successes. Every now and then I was able to take the Wellington teacher to meet 'their' family for the first time — the emotion, the joy and the mutual knowledge displayed on these visits indicated that the relationship that had been built could be described as both meaningful and loving.

This wonderfully positive and successful situation was far from universal. I spent an afternoon with people who were about to sail around the world with their eight- and ten-year-old children. They wanted TCS work, and it was my task to show them how to operate things. It seemed clear, however, that they would have trouble instilling good sailing behaviour, and the likelihood of the children getting stuck up the mast or falling overboard seemed very high. I suggested they view safety as the primary learning task and get back to me when the kids were sufficiently boat-trained for reading, writing and maths to be deemed important again. They didn't, nor did they return any work to their teachers in Wellington. I trust this is not because they had drowned.

I loved going to Great Barrier Island. The 'going' was always special. In the first two years the only flights were with Seabee Air. This was a small company that operated ageing amphibious Gruman Widgens. On my first-ever flight I sat strapped into an unpadded seat in the no-frills, unlined interior, senses on high alert, noting everything I could. This included four rivets that were revolving and rattling. The noise was excitingly loud as the plane crashed through waves in its struggle to get airborne. I marvelled at its seaworthiness, and remember, with words like 'doomed' wanting to be part of this description, one landing, if that's the right word, on Auckland Harbour on a stormy day. As the waves literally broke over the cabin top, I discovered that the word 'amphibious' could encompass aspects of submarine behaviour. But I loved it, just as I had loved the small planes that started to fly between Savai'i and Apia, eliminating the time and fear generated by the va'a kelosini.

The first of these planes in Sāmoa was a comfortable and fast six-seater Cessna. Siainiu and I got to know the young New Zealand pilot, Chris, well. I would try to maximise my time in Apia and would often catch the last plane back to Savai'i. On these flights Chris would let me 'fly', a process that mainly involved trying to compensate for the unequal weights of the wingtip fuel tanks and keep the plane level. Once he said he would perform a manoeuvre, and that when he yelled 'Now!' I was to point to the sky. He duly put the plane through a series of loops, spirals and slides, and I lost all sense of direction, something he admitted tended to happen to him as well. After a year of operation, the company purchased two Fletcher topdressing aircraft which they fitted with two rows of very small seats facing each other. The small size of the cabin meant that passengers could fit only if they shared the same leg space. I once flew with the pastor's somewhat corpulent wife. Her ample buttocks meant she was well forward in the seat and our legs were intertwined with an involuntary intimacy that was enhanced every time the plane lurched or bumped. There were no windows, but we steadfastly gazed out of them anyway.

When I caught the first flight in the morning and was the only passenger, Chris would try to break his short take-off record. A white-painted stone was placed beside the unpaved runway to mark the previous record, and a ground-staff member would be at the ready (if his unprotected ears allowed coherent thought) to move the stone to mark the new record and signal to Chris that this had now been achieved and he could settle down a bit. Take-off involved revving the engine to its shuddering maximum, doing the aviation equivalent of suddenly letting in the clutch, and spurring the overlarge topdressing engine to hurl the plane into the air. As soon as the plane left the ground, Chris would throw it into a right-hand turn, wings at ninety degrees to the ground, machine and bodies shuddering with the g-forces this generated. Chris would grin and yahoo at each new record, and did not think me yelling that he was a crazy stupid bastard was appropriate congratulation. This service folded shortly after we left Savai'i, much to the relief of the pastor's wife and those who lived nearby.

This background prepared me well for the Seabee flights to Great Barrier. I remember, however, a middle-aged woman I once travelled with — seated beside her, I hasten to add. She was going, for the first time, to visit her daughter who had recently moved to Great Barrier 'to live in a hovel in the bush with a hippie man, unkempt of appearance and speech'. She did not approve of him, nor her daughter who had had such a promising career in pharmaceutical sales. She did not like anything she had heard of Great Barrier life, but she was going to try to make the best of things. She had a large cake in a white cardboard box sitting on her lap. A cake that was to symbolise her forgiveness, achieve reconciliation and her daughter's possible return to the mainland and mainstream thinking. The plane terrified her to the point of teetering on the edge of swoon for the entire journey. I rejected her judgements but felt genuinely sorry for her fear.

We landed, after a series of swoops, sudden losses of altitude and considerable shuddering. She praised all known deities when the plane settled into the calm waters and taxied to the shore. I then had to tell her that we had arrived at Port Fitzroy and that her daughter lived at Tryphena. We would have to take off again, fly to the other end of the island and lurch down to Tryphena's rougher waters. As I gave out this dread news, she stared at me in horror, and her hands, unconsciously I think, slowly crushed the cake box so that rich chocolate icing oozed between her shaking fingers.

THERE WERE THREE primary schools on the island but no secondary school. This meant that the few primary-aged children I saw lived in very remote places. I loved visiting these children and aimed to see them once every term — these were still the days of three-term years. The few hours spent walking through the bush to get to their various dwellings always felt like a bonus. I was being paid by the taxpayers to go tramping.

I admit that in the early days, some of this tramping was in vain and I became lost, but, as I had found in Sāmoa, you can't stay lost for long on an island. Sāmoans have two main directions. One is *i uta*, inland; the other *gatai*, towards the sea. I don't think they have an expression for my frequent error — walking in circles. Sometimes, it wasn't my fault. People would have given me instructions like 'You walk along the beach, then, at the big tree you go inland.' There would be many big trees and it was hard to know which one was 'the big tree'.

I would hide a good walking stick in the bushes at the beginning of some of the more challenging tracks, like the steep one to Rosalie Bay. It was always reassuring to find these sticks waiting for me. They made me feel I knew what I was doing. Everyone else, of course, knew what I was doing. Some maintained that the TCS job was just a cover and I was really a drug courier with licence to wander to out-of-the-way places. This was said with a smile, but with a little seriousness just in case I could offer any services.

Some places I went to had been set up in a rush of 1980s hippie enthusiasm. People used up a lot of this enthusiasm lugging timber for miles through the bush. Some 'houses' were, at best, primitive. I knew one family, two adults and two children, who lived in a shelter made of two sheets of black polythene, one on the ground and the other stretched above, between two trees. Cooking would almost always be over a fire, and I admit that I developed a genuine liking for spinach and lentils cooked over an open fire, eaten out of a pottery bowl, crouched under a canvas too old and tired to keep battling with the rain. More often than it should have been, there would be a tired woman with too many kids trying to wash clothes in a cold creek, and a man with long hair and skinny cigarettes explaining the underlying philosophy to me.

One of the purposes of my job was to explain the realities of living situations to teachers in Wellington. It was sometimes hard to do this patiently when I saw the work of children who had to struggle to get anything done rejected because of a lingering odour of smoke or smears of mud. A few teachers were convinced that students who submitted smoke-flavoured pages were guilty of not trying, or even deliberate acts of insolence, and refused to mark their work.

I encountered one extraordinary case in which a teacher had been able to exert negativity of such power that her words, written in Wellington, produced fear and despondency when they were read on Great Barrier Island. The pupil concerned was fourteen-year-old Mary, living with her mother and sister in a series of tents on a remote part of the island. I had to squeeze into Mary's tent, stretching muscles not really stretched since sitting cross-legged in Sāmoa. There was the need not to touch the walls of the tent, lest their last vestiges of waterproofing succumb to the inevitable rain. It was not comfortable. This discomfort was dramatically increased by Mary clutching her schoolwork to herself, crying and saying she couldn't show it to me because, if she did, I would know what a bad person she was.

After a lot of talk and caution – don't touch the tent, don't touch the child, don't submit to your legs' threat of cramp – she passed the folder to me, head down, distraught. The work she had done was good. Not great and clearly in need of some adult input, but a serious attempt at producing what was needed. There were quirky illustrations, some good ideas and an obvious investment of time. This was work deserving praise and encouragement, all the more so because of the difficult conditions under which it had been produced. There were no comments from her teacher, but the script was liberally scattered with red stars made with a stamp, each star looking a bit like insignia on a Chinese army truck.

I told Mary her work was great, that she must have worked very hard. I referred to particular parts of the work that were particularly good – I had discovered, sometime earlier, that if you want to praise an insecure teenager at, say, Force Seven, then the praise has to be delivered at least Force Twenty.

She looked away and passed me some letters from her teacher. They were poisonous pools of negativity, subtle and clever. They would have taken time to write, to refine the intention to condemn and harm. Their spell had travelled intact from a desk in Wellington to a pup tent up a muddy Great Barrier track, their malice increasing along the way. The vast majority of TCS students, and their families, love the feedback they get from teachers; the arrival of a new posting is usually a moment of joy and anticipation. For Mary this had been replaced by dread — justifiable dread. In a desperate attempt to find something positive I pointed out all the red stars. Mary's weeping increased — it appeared that red stars were a secret code for *This is especially displeasing*.

I berated Mary's mother, reminding her that part of the TCS deal was that parents take an active part in their child's schooling and do enough reading of the work to know the challenges their child faces, how they have responded to them and what the teacher has thought of it all. A big demand but, had she done it, she would have saved her daughter agonies that may well have had a lifelong effect.

A new teacher, one who bubbled with the joy of learning and the delight of being with children, was organised. The original teacher ceased teaching. She was an unhappy person who had faced horrible health challenges alone, and had allowed herself to take things out on an uncertain teenager living in the smallest of tents in a remote backwater. I hope, in the end, she understood the destructive power of her words, but more than that I hope Mary had sufficient youthful resistance to bounce back.

On my next visit to the island, the family had packed up their tents and left.

WHEN I WENT to Great Barrier, I stayed at the famous Bob and Tipi's guest house in Tryphena. The house was a large, sprawling affair, warm and welcoming. Tipi was the same, and we became friends and confidants, sitting up late at night and telling each other our life stories. She was also an invaluable source of inside information — I often arrived at homes with far more information than I really needed. She was a superb and generous cook, and as part of the accommodation deal she would pack a lunch for me. Somehow, when she knew I was visiting people who were struggling to eat anything more than spinach and lentils, my lunch would be three times its usual size.

Tipi died some years ago. The whole island mourned.

There are many tales that could be told about Great Barrier. It was, and still is, that sort of place. I met many people there doing their best and trying to work out new ways of living. I also met people locked into the complexities of living in a small, isolated place — complexities that resulted in forgiveness and, in many cases, refusal to forgive. Life for many was hard.

I would, at times, be overwhelmed by the needs of my students, particularly the secondary students, who were so often stalled by what seemed to them to be insurmountable hurdles that would quickly have disappeared if there had been a teacher available to look over their shoulders and nudge them back to the right track. I wondered about parents who had made the choice to live on Great Barrier but had not fully considered the implications for their children.

I never fully managed to convince parents that making their child stay in his or her room for five hours every day was not enough, especially if they had no knowledge of what their child was doing. Many kids sat out their five hours without opening a TCS booklet. They read books, doodled endless pictures — one girl showed me an alarmingly detailed pencil sketch of her body with red crosses showing the sites of the piercings she was going to get done as soon as she escaped to the mainland. Some slept through their five hours; most dreamed. Cell phones and laptops, both of which would have been their salvation, were not yet freely available.

The sword of Damocles that hung over many of their heads was the looming School Certificate exams. They knew they would be found out, that their failure would be condemned by their mystified parents who thought they had done everything right. I organised parents' meetings, and in a desperate effort to get the message across set up role-plays of good and bad pupil supervision. They thought I was a good actor but wondered if what I was on about had anything to do with them.

I ranted about the Ministry of Education not seeing fit to build and staff a secondary school. The three primary schools on the island had their ups and downs but gave splendid service. It is hard to escape the question of how the students there were to be catered for once their primary education finished — a question that sadly remains unanswered today. TCS does great work, but it is not the ideal package for many, if not most, students. I advocated as strongly as I could for a secondary school to be built. I see now that my case was undermined by my failure to fully disguise my desire to run such a school.

14.

THE BULK OF my work was in Auckland City with kids enrolled at TCS because some kind of problem prevented them from going to school. A number of these enrolments were of pregnant schoolgirls. I feel uncomfortable placing pregnancy in the problem category, but it cannot be denied that whatever joy is associated with bringing new life into the world, doing so brought sadness and challenge to many of these young women. In some cases, it produced a burning ambition to do well with schoolwork, a determination not to fall behind peers still at school. There was no doubt that these students were going to do well, but for many others the challenges of pregnancy were overwhelming, and school seemed to hold little relevance.

I think we all knew there were huge cultural divisions in Auckland. Divisions of wealth — the have-yachts and the have-nots. Lack of money was evident each winter when I went into houses with no heating, the kids wrapped in blankets as they tried to work at their desks. Jan worked on the North Shore, and in the four years of my employment with TCS she did not encounter one student who was going to keep her baby. I worked in South Auckland and I did not encounter one student who was not going to keep her baby. I found this statistic remarkable and sad. All the young women I met invested whatever they could in preparation for the baby's arrival. They showed me clothes, second-hand cots, prams that needed just a little bit of repair, and posters they had made using the TCS art kit saying, 'Welcome my darling, darling baby!' There was lots of pink and lots of lace.

Very few of these young women had any real support. Most lived at home with their parents, doing daily penance in an endless series of domestic tasks. Some, I suspected, were being sexually exploited, but no one ever confirmed this. I would express worries to TCS, but would be told my task was teaching, not counselling. (Huh? Can you teach without counselling?)

I think the biggest sadness was visiting after babies had been born. So often the pink-and-lace dreams had been shattered by the realities of baby care, sleepless nights and worries about money. Babies would become the responsibility of the whole family, would toddle about in regimes that would have won Vaifou's approval. Of course, I am generalising here – generalising and being afraid. My knowledge of families was limited by the infrequency of my visits and by the fact that most young mums didn't return any work and were, accordingly, removed from the roll. To those who don't have, more shall be taken away.

There were bright spots, candles of optimism surviving in

the wind. In one case, the lad who had fathered the child took full responsibility for his part in the situation. He was a smiling fifteen-year-old, and he made TCS history by demanding to be enrolled in the pregnancy category. He and his girlfriend would do their schoolwork together, monitoring each other and demanding more work be done. When I visited there would be laughter and the tears of laughter as they told me about each other's shortcomings:

'He can't spell for shit, Tim, and he doesn't always check even when he knows he's wrong – he's real hard to teach.'

'She looks at the back of the book for the maths answers. I know she does cos she can't talk about it, you know, discuss how she arrived at the answer. Don't think she knows her tables even – she's real hard to teach.'

They would describe their Friday afternoon trips to the Post Office. They regarded the sending of their bags of finished work back to TCS as occasions for ceremony, celebration and KFC on the way home. As I write this, I feel a strong and emotional hope that their optimism, courage, good cheer and abundant love for each other have survived.

I remember one young mother in particular. She was an excellent student, organised, intelligent, hardworking. Her schoolwork and her baby thrived. The house where she lived was basic and cold. It was, on some visits, full of people; at other times it would be only her and baby. She would talk lots about the future, the exams she was going to pass and how she would become a teacher.

One day her form teacher rang me and said the usual steady flow of work had dried up and the student was not answering his phone calls and letters. I made a rushed home visit. One look at her let me know something had changed. She knew why I was there and why I was looking at her, searching for words. She, seated at her desk surrounded by unfinished work, glanced up at me, clearly disciplining the tears that wanted to spill from her eyes.

'Those Mongrel Mobs,' she said. 'They're real bad buggers.'

Courage and optimism often seemed the only thing some people had in their struggle to get ahead. I went to one Ōtara house and noticed a certificate of some sort framed on the wall. As I bent closer to read it, the student's mother said, 'Yeah, I know. That's my oldest daughter's School Certificate exam entry slip. She didn't pass anything, but she was the first one to get to sit the exam and we're proud of her.'

At least NCEA would have given this student something to show what she could do, something to put on the wall. Enough for now — I will tilt at the examination windmill in a later chapter.

I visited one student, a tough little nut expelled from school. Another student, Hemi, from up the road, was there. Hemi was a well-organised rough diamond, getting through his schoolwork and earning a considerable amount of money using his size and strength working on a casual basis for a furniture-removal company. I encountered a lot of furniture-shifting being done by young out-of-school South Auckland lads on an informal, under-the-table basis. Some days I thought this was opportunity, some days I thought this was exploitation. Hemi had taken his neighbour under his wing and was getting him organised. He seemed to be doing an excellent job. I was flattered and amused to hear him using several of my phrases and words, although I couldn't help hearing, in some of them, a ring of pomposity and fatuousness. Hemi was, indeed, teaching both of us.

He had, however, a phrase of his own that he used repeatedly – *all that shit*, as in 'We posted his English, and all that shit, yesterday; I put his maths, and all that shit, in the red box; I make him sit in that chair and read his set texts and all that shit; we're gonna do heaps of work and sit School Cert and all that shit ...' I do hope the system that expelled Hemi from school, presumably for his bad language and all that shit, later came to see his brilliance as a teacher and his kindness to his peers.

Itinerant students formed an interesting and diverse group. Some of them were travellers, but most saw this as a category that would open TCS doors. There were people who lived in motionless buses but who promised to have it towed to the next town if that was what I needed. There were circus children, happier to show me new tricks than schoolwork. And then there were the Believers.

Some of the Believers had their own religious faith and sought TCS as a refuge from the evils their children would be exposed to at day school. They tended to see me as an ally, a collaborator in their desire for protection. Most balanced their statements of faith, and their judgement about the evil of others, with the lies they told about their travel itineraries. Again, if a child was learning and seemed happy, I did not rock their ark. If there was obvious unhappiness and an absence of schoolwork, I would agonise over whether to 'report them'. I have long wondered about the power this phrase seems to hold in New Zealand. In most cases there isn't anyone to report them to and, if there was, the likelihood of that person taking action is usually fairly slender. Nonetheless, the threat of 'reporting' often resulted in a much-improved flow of schoolwork.

Other Believers had their own educational creed that could be successfully pursued only at home. These folk ranged from dedicated, forward-thinking, enlightened hard-working parents to the chap who thought his daughter's education would become adequate only if she stayed home and read the complete works of P G Wodehouse. The dilemma, in many cases, was that however legitimate the students' enrolment status was, it was generally better if they were on our roll than if they took the next step and became registered as home schoolers.

In theory, to be granted school exemption and to home-school a child, a parent needs to submit a detailed plan of how they are going to implement the curriculum. They also have to accept regular visits from the Ministry of Education. In practice, however, it seems very difficult for these visits to take place, and I saw a number of children who ended up locked into some pretty peculiar sets of beliefs. There are always people who know the system and are able to ensure they get their own way, even if their way is a little crazy.

If this chapter is becoming a bit of a hotch-potch of anecdotes and experiences, this in many ways reflects the TCS experience. The work involved lots of travel, trying to keep effective contact with too many students. My basic roll was around two hundred, but there was a turnover of at least fifty per cent. In other words, the total contact group was around three hundred. These numbers were difficult to manage because of the high percentage of first visits, with the multiplicity of resources and tasks to be organised. Often I sensed that if I didn't move slowly and gently, the fish would shun the bait and never be seen again. This meant that several 'first visits' had to be made to ensure that the student became organised and under way.

My South Island colleagues spoke of the frustrations of working with parents who had supervised TCS for years and felt they not only knew the ropes but also knew the errors in the ropes and how they needed to be rearranged. These folks wanted little from the RR beyond being told they were doing a wonderful job. I wanted some of these parents, but think I only ever met two.

What I did meet was a wide variety of people. I remember many of them clearly. There was the solo mum on an island with a free-range child and a 'library' consisting only of hundreds of Mills & Boon books. There were couples in remote places with relationship problems. One of them would ask me to meet them in the washhouse for a furious discussion of the iniquities of the other, followed by the other making the same request. The instruction not to try to be a counsellor would ring in my ears. I ignored it. These people had no one else to talk with. One such family achieved an effective and lasting reconciliation – we would joke, when I arrived on subsequent visits, about whether a trip to the washhouse was necessary.

I remember a student who lived with her grandfather in a hut on the shores of the Kaipara Harbour. The three-hour trek along the beach to get there, the length of the visit and the start of the return trek had to be carefully timed around tide times. On more than one occasion they walked back with me for an hour or two so we could finish maths questions before the water cut off access.

Another student lived at the end of the Poutu Peninsula. I would ring her up from Dargaville to check she was home and willing to see me before driving the winding hour-long drive to her place. Each time she reassured me she would be there, that she had done 'heaps of schoolwork' and she was looking forward to seeing me. Almost every time I got there her mum would say, in a more matter-of-fact way than I wished, 'Nah, sorry, she's buggered off down the paddocks somewhere.' The final score, at the end of four years was: The Paddocks 6, TCS 2.

I saw a father and his son in the city. He was a large man with strong ideas about Māori sovereignty and a reputation for not letting representatives of any government department on his property. For some reason we got on well, despite me being in the pay of the government. His son was an intelligent boy, working well and with a hunger for learning. He seemed to greatly enjoy the political chats he had with his father. I resolved to find time for them – to do so seemed more worthwhile than driving up and down the Poutu Peninsula. I listened to the father's ideas; some contained exciting political visions, some seemed to have the seeds of paranoia. Over the years, many of these seeds took root and flourished, became a forest shading out his capacity for debate. On what turned out to be my last visit he was deeply distressed. He waved a *Playboy* magazine in my face.

'Look,' he cried. 'Look at the lengths my enemies, the agents of this fascist state, will go to corrupt my son! They have planted this magazine in the hope he will look at it and his mind will become poisoned.'

The son glanced at me, imploring me not to say anything, not to suggest that his hunger for knowledge may have extended past the material TCS could provide. I didn't dob him in, but after considerable agonising I knew I had to 'report' the father's condition. He did receive help, or at least offers of help, but he never let me on the property again.

I worried about children who had been diagnosed as having some personality or learning difficulty but were trapped at home with the root source of that difficulty. I also worried about the large and growing number of fourteen- and fifteen-year-olds who were out of school. If a child is to be expelled from school, a certain number of actions should be put in place. These include notifying the Ministry, notifying the parents (this didn't happen, by the way, when my son Pete was expelled from Mount Albert Grammar in 1989), and making some attempt to find another school willing to take the student. For many schools this was all too difficult, and what became known as 'Kiwi suspension' took place – i.e. the kid was told to go away and not come back, end of story … and formal education … and, in many cases, hope for the future.

It is an easy trap to be judgemental about these schools, to think they could have tried harder and been more liberal. But I also know that a school without boundaries and expectations soon descends into chaos. I don't want to teach kids whose active disruption, swearing, sexism, racism and violence prevents others from learning, from being happy and safe at school. When I met students guilty of all these things, and more, in their homes, away from their peers and the institutions they had come to hate, it was sometimes easy to establish rapport, to be on their side. It is such a dilemma, such an impasse. Several times I persuaded schools to take students back. In some cases they were expelled again within a week.

TCS was not, with a few notable exceptions, the answer. Unless there was real support at home, or the student had exceptional ability and motivation, the TCS enrolment was little more than a costly exercise to allow schools to say, 'We have done something and it's over to them to make the most of the opportunity.'

I wrote a short story in which I tried to amalgamate elements of the tales the many 'excluded' students I met had told me. 'Told' is probably the wrong word. They let things slip, blurted the odd confession, had faces and bruises that were more articulate than their words. This is not the story of one student, but all the elements of the story, damn it, are true.

Home Schooling

My schoolwork book is about the monarch butterfly.

I am sitting at the kitchen table with the spilled sugar and jam. They told me to wipe the table clean, but I didn't, because I like the sugar and jam. When I move the books I feel the sugar. Sometimes, ants come. I give them names. They have races. If my special one wins, I won't have to go to the garage.

I am not allowed to go to school because I am stubborn and disobedient.

Uncle makes me read the Principal's letter every day.

The letter says:

> *I have to inform you that recently Charlie has displayed consistent disobedience and bad behaviour, culminating in the assault of a teacher. Accordingly, he has been suspended from this school, pending a meeting of the Board's Disciplinary sub-committee.*
>
> *In Years Nine and Ten he showed that he was a clever boy, capable of academic and sporting success. Some staff considered that he had leadership potential. It saddens me, personally, that he has decided, this year, to do little work, become non-compliant and make unwise friendship choices.*

Me, Grandma and Uncle, we went to the meeting about me, at the school. We waited, sitting in the corridor, with Uncle going 'bloody schools', his arms on his knees and his breath getting deeper, looking at me and saying, 'You!'

In the room they didn't say sorry about the waiting, but a Māori man said a prayer in his language, and a woman I'd never seen before kissed Grandma and called her Auntie. The Deputy Principal was there and he called me Charlie. First time he'd called me Charlie. Usually called me my Grandma's name. Or said 'You', like Uncle.

He said, 'Hello, Charlie,' and then didn't talk to me. He had a red book, with 'Incident Book' written on it in black felt-tip pen. He read from the book: 'On 4 February, Charlie refused to leave the Science class. Remained seated, threw science equipment onto the floor. He refused to clean up. Silent and surly. I was summoned to remove him.'

Yes, Mr Deputy Principal, Sir, you removed me. Took me past Kitione's mates, so they couldn't get me, that day. I made the finger sign at them, behind your back. Is that in your red book?

The Deputy Principal wrote on the whiteboard. He put a dot in front of each line, like this:

- 5 February: fighting with Kitione
- 9, 10, 11 Feb: wagging
- 12 Feb: threw stones at Kitione; spoke to me, in his home language, definitely derogatory. Refused to come to office or talk with counsellor
- 13 Feb: struck teacher. Suspended.

When he finished writing, he pressed a button and printed pages of the words came out. I thought this was amazing. Grandma and Uncle were given copies. Grandma said thank you a lot of times; Uncle pointed his copy at me.

'You,' he said, his teeth together. 'You!'

The Deputy Principal asked me if I wanted to say anything. I asked him how the whiteboard works. He sighed.

The lady who called Grandma Auntie spoke to me in a soft voice, her mouth smiling, her words so gentle it was like it was just the two of us. Her words were about love and forgiveness and Grandma's sacrifice and getting older and our people and achievement. My eyes felt the prickly feeling, so I softly made the shape of some words, just for the two of us. The words were 'Fuck off, arse lady, fuck off!'

She jerked away, teeth clamped, like Uncle's.

I didn't listen much any more. The bits I did hear, I wrote down on a whiteboard inside my head:

- non-compliant
- exclusion
- anger management
- standards

When it was all over, Grandma said: 'Sorry and thank you, and sorry for him.'

Uncle said: 'I know my duty. My Bible tells me my duty.'

The people in the room understood and looked down. The Deputy Principal said, 'Well, at the end of the day, it's a cultural thing, isn't it?'

They shook our hands and looked at the next family, waiting in the corridor.

Uncle beat me with the wood till Grandma cried for him to stop. I crawled to my mattress and lay there with the words from the whiteboard going past my eyes:

- anger management
- standards
- exclusion

I didn't understand them, but you need words to help you climb around the pain. Most times, I use numbers. Sometimes people's names. Say them slowly and breathe and then start to test each hurting part. Say them slowly and play the pictures through your head. You on the floor, Uncle like a mountain, the sound of the stick, your voice howling. Uncle yelling: 'You, why you howl like a dog? You hush the noise!'

- anger management
- standards
- future

I think it's only bruises, and I sleep and don't even know if Grandma comes in to see me.

My schoolwork arrives two weeks later. Uncle says I must work for six hours each day. I stay here at the table with the monarch butterflies and the ants, the white-board filling up and emptying.

My book says:

The Monarch Butterfly. Order LEPIDOPTERA, Family Nymphalidae.

All day I say these words as the clock moves. When Uncle comes home and asks if I left the table and what I learnt today, I say LEPIDOPTERA, in a big voice because it is capitals, and Nymph . . . I can't say the whole word, but Uncle doesn't know.

He says, 'Good, you keep the learning every day.'

The next morning, I read:

> *In summer this beautiful butterfly flies about looking for a mate and a place to lay eggs.*

I think of my mates and running with them when we are in trouble or trying to get someone. Running together, fast and laughing, our feet flying. I smile and draw a picture, on the book, of the sign we put on the walls. It is like a butterfly with sharp corners. The clock moves from 9.30 to 11.00 while I make this picture.

Uncle sees it and punches my ear.

> *Caterpillars feed on swan plants* (Asclepias physocarpa) *and have five stages before they reach their full length of 55mm (fig A).*

Fig A shows a fat caterpillar. I draw this caterpillar, then rub it out.

> *Then suddenly their voracious feeding stops . . .*

I say 'voracious' and let it be written on the whiteboard over and over again. I don't know its meaning, but I like it. I say it to Uncle. He likes it, too.

> *Then suddenly their voracious feeding stops and they wander off, searching for a suitable site to pupate.*

They hang upside down and then suddenly shed their skin and transform into a pupa (fig B).

I know what this means because it shows me in fig B. A dark thing, wrapped up, changing inside. Hanging quietly from the branch and changing.

About three weeks later the pupa darkens. Soon the adult butterfly emerges.

That night, my mates come to the window. I jump outside and run with them. We see the cars parked in the dark part and use the stone to break the windows. We take money and cigarettes. And bottles of wine. An alarm starts. We run again, laughing and so fast. No one can catch us, ever.

The next street, wanting more, shouting when we find something good. Nothing good in the car we are in when the cops come. They yell, 'You little black bastard, what the fuck do you think you're doing?'

They only catch me and Siaki. I'm happy the others get away and laugh. The cop looks around, then kicks my leg. We go to the police station. People come and say: 'Yes, that's my coat, all right, but what about the damage, what about the bloody damage? So pointless!'

The cops want names. We say nothing. They bang the table but don't kick. I don't say my name or where I live, so they ring the Youth Aid man and he comes and says that's Charlie and gives Uncle's name. They ring Uncle and he comes and picks me up. It is three o'clock in the morning and we don't see anyone else on the road.

Uncle says no words. He stops the car and grabs my arm. He throws me down and kicks. He picks me up and throws me into the house. Grandma comes in. She has the broom.

'I wash my hands, boy, I wash my hands!' she says, crying and hitting. 'Nobody can fix you, nothing.'

She goes away and leaves me with Uncle.

When light comes back in my head, I am outside. This time I know parts of me are broken. The whiteboard can't stay still in my mind. Words, where are my words? I try:

- voracious
- lepidoptera
- transform

They have grown big and my lips can only move over half of them, so I go back to:

- one
- two
- three

I am only at eight when I reach the garage.

The ladder, the rope. It is hard, with only one arm working and the sharp stabs in my stomach, but my words come back:

198

- I wash my hands
- nothing can fix you
- Grandma don't be the one hitting me

The ladder goes.
  The pupa darkens.

If there is an answer to kids who don't fit into schools, then it is an answer with many elements — poverty, violence at home, bad hearing, bad nutrition, lack of language skills, bad friends, and the total unsuitability of our school structures for all but those who already have everything in their favour. As a teacher there seemed little I could do about most of these things. As a teacher I found myself thinking, at times quite desperately, about the last item. We had to find ways of rejecting the gifts and structures of the damned nineteenth-century British missionaries.

Not all TCS work was like this, but I knew I did not want to continue working in this way, becoming aware of problems but being unable to do much about them. I was in danger of becoming a teacher concerned with academic progress and nothing else. I found myself longing for continuity of contact with students, to be there to witness the miracle of young children learning to read. I also, in an uncertain and unformed kind of way, wondered if I could put my ideas about changing the structure of a school in place. I also knew I had to be home full-time and work on my relationship — it had been on life-support for far too long.

As all these thoughts pounded around my head, I saw, in November 1987, the principal's position at Newton Central

School advertised. It was what I wanted, truly, madly, deeply. I was ready to forsake the glamour of gumboots on Great Barrier, Tipi's large lunches and long chats, the highly sociable trips to Wellington and the endless report writing. I wanted to be at a school where I could go every day, plant things and watch them grow. I had jumped through all the multi-coloured hoops of the grading system and had all the numbers.

I wrote myself up as the best person to lead this ailing little inner-city multicultural primary school. I pulled out all the stops, and even a tie from my bottom drawer, and went for it. In the middle of the job interview, I caught myself talking with more passion than the panel were probably used to but I thought, bugger it, they might as well know how I feel.

I won the job.

Later, Roberta, the school secretary and school committee member who had been on the interview panel, told me I was the only applicant who'd seemed enthusiastic about working specifically at Newton Central. The others, she said, had impressive qualifications, had spoken about wanting to be principals, but in a generalised sense. Later, when we had a board of trustees empowered with making appointments, I was astonished by how few applicants had done any research about the school or attempted to outline how they saw their strengths fitting the specific needs of Newton Central. I kept being reminded of a certain famous concrete contractor who had allegedly said, 'I want to be mayor, I don't care where.'

15.

NEWTON CENTRAL SCHOOL was established in 1924 on the steep slopes of the city side of Newton Gully. At that time Newton was a populous suburb already contributing to two other schools, Newton East and Newton West. Newton Central is the only one surviving today. In those days you could walk down the gully from Great North Road, cross the stream at the bottom and work your way up past a mixture of villas and workers' cottages to New North Road. This became an impossible walk in the 1950s when the construction of the North-Western motorway along the gully floor began. It is hard to imagine a more dramatic and clumsy implement for social change.

This motorway gobbled up houses, separated the two sides of the gully and increased noise levels. The Southern Motorway development similarly bisected a suburb, but was topped with a noise-reducing smooth seal. The Ministry of Works, and the agencies into which it subsequently transmogrified, deemed the households and school of the Newton area to be of lesser importance, and less likely to be able to organise an effective fuss, so the North-Western was sealed in the less-expensive stone chip. The community became divided, literally; houses were lost and the area was subjected to a constant, fatiguing background motorway noise. As one resident said, 'The sound is the roar of surf breaking on our grief.'

The school has been rebuilt three times. Initially, there were wooden buildings in the same style as the old Bayfield School in Jervois Road. In the 1920s these were replaced with two large concrete rectangles, echoing and Dickensian. These gloomy and draughty buildings were in turn replaced in the 1970s by a series of quite low weatherboard-clad classrooms and a new administration block. To my eye, these buildings, especially the administration block, looked more like a series of houses than an institution. The buildings were pleasing, but the surrounding land, unplanted and steep, was in desperate need of the softening effect of trees and flowers.

From the time I first went there, and for the ten years I was principal, I would often walk around the grounds early in the morning, or at night, hugging myself with the joy of having the running of this place entrusted to me. I would walk slowly, enjoying the quietness that comes over a school when everyone has gone home, planning what to plant, what to change both in the grounds and in the hearts and minds of those who came here to learn and to teach.

I had wanted to start my time as principal slowly, to observe and ponder before planting anything. I think I had thirty minutes on my first day when I sat at my desk wondering what to do. The immediacy of day-to-day demands and decisions quickly intruded, and the question for the next ten years was not so much what to do but how to fit everything in.

The first of these intrusions came early on the Friday afternoon of Week One. A teacher came to me and said, 'I'm just going down the road to get the video.'

'What video?' I asked.

'Dunno,' she replied. 'Anything will do. We always combine classes and keep them quiet with a video on Friday afternoons.'

'No,' I said, 'no, I don't like that at all.'

I didn't expect this to make any difference, but she went back to the other waiting teachers with the news that I had banned videos.

Pius Blank, from Beresford Street and Mount Albert days, had rung me up when he first learned of my appointment, full of words of congratulation and advice. His final comment was: 'However, now you are principal of a city school you should remind yourself, every night when you lay your head on the pillow to go to sleep, that there is someone, somewhere, pissed off with you.' That Friday night, his words gained a haunting veracity.

I had already had a taste of how challenging issues could arise and quickly have a profound influence on relationships long before the 1988 school year began. The first of these came when members of the school committee told me they believed the chairman had absconded with funds. They alleged that he had taken money collected at the end-of-year school concert home for safekeeping over the weekend. When he delivered the money to the school on the Monday, it was well short of the previously calculated amount. The concert had consisted of dances from each island group, and parents would have come forward and placed money not just on their own children but on the children of relatives and friends. People gave not from their excess but from their sufficiency, and I am sure each concert was followed by a lean week or two. The amount each group raised was announced publicly and with pride. Sadly, in this instance, the amount delivered to the school did not equate to the sum of the parts. I knew the person concerned and had spoken with him about the school, and my desire to be there, well before the appointment interview. I had liked him and looked forward to working with him. He wouldn't talk about the missing money, but very soon sold his house and went elsewhere, leaving behind a cloud that never fully disappeared.

The second major challenge centred around a group wanting to establish a Māori language school. This group was led by a high-powered couple, both lecturing at Auckland University, both determined that their children would grow up as speakers of te reo. The problem was that although they had secured buildings in another school and a commitment from the Education Department to pay teacher salaries, they were not allowed to set up as an independent school. They had to enter a 'big brother' relationship with an established school, to become what was known as a 'side school' of that school. All schools they had approached, including the 'host' school, had refused to accept what they thought might be a dodgy arrangement – there was still an attitude of 'You never knew what them Maoris are going to do.' I had no difficulty in accepting this hosting role and in persuading my school committee to agree to it. In fact, the arrangement demanded very little time, the occasional signature and a lot of pleasantness. Very soon, the introduction of Tomorrow's Schools meant the 'side school' was given the independence it should have had in the beginning.

I have two clear memories about the negotiations for this arrangement. The initial meeting was called by the Inspectorate. It was held at Newton Central and attended by several inspectors, one of whom ran the meeting. It was also attended by the parents who wanted to establish the side school, their kaumātua and me. The kaupapa of the meeting was 100 per cent Pākehā – no greetings, no karakia, no cup of tea. When it was over and the inspectors had left, the kaumātua asked if he could say a final karakia, despite the fact the horses had bolted.

I raged about the way things had been conducted, my rage fuelled by the realisation that I should have claimed host rights and done things differently but hadn't thought quickly or bravely enough to do so. One of the parents put her hand on my shoulder and told me to be more patient. 'We, after all,' she said, 'have had to be patient for more than a hundred and fifty years.'

The school roll when I arrived was exactly one hundred, about 30 per cent of the school's capacity. Only two of those one hundred children were Pākehā; the rest were of Māori and Pacific Island origin. The smattering of Chinese and Indian children who had been at Beresford Street were not there. Their parents had prospered and moved on. I was happy to run a school that had only non-European children, but I was very unhappy to have a school that did not represent the demography of the neighbourhood.

Statistics and observation, much aided by the fact that I lived in Kingsland, part of the school's catchment, told me the community was mixed and at least 50 per cent of it was Pākehā. These people took their children elsewhere. They 'knew' Newton Central was a bad school, full of violence, low levels of learning, lazy teachers, child abuse, drugs, witchcraft, black magic, scabies and head lice. None of them had visited the school or come to talk with me about it. They had gleaned their information from bars and coffee shops, from conversations over the back fence and from a friend whose great-aunt had been there thirty years ago. I found changing the reputation of the school a bit like steering a giant tanker at sea — I could make what felt like all the right moves in the wheelhouse, but it was a long time before the ship began to change direction.

MY FIRST FEW YEARS were a mixture of jubilation and despair. The jubilation centred on the high standard of much of the teaching and being with children on a consistent day-to-day basis. I felt I came to know something about all of them, their names and their families. Admittedly, learning names had become a more difficult task as society was changing — it used to be that when John Smith married Mary, she took his name, and they came to school to enrol a series of little Smiths. This simplicity, with its implications and pitfalls, was replaced by an increasingly complex array of double-barrelled surnames, children in the same family taking either their mother's name or their father's name, blended families, single-parent families, and people who had selected a name at random from the phone book. I did eventually come to grips with these complexities, but don't regard this as a great achievement — there were only about a hundred of them.

So much centred on getting more people to see that the school was a safe and worthwhile place to send their children. At the beginning of my second year, I looked forward with excitement to an influx of new children. By ten o'clock on the first morning of the term there were more enrolments — three of them, offset by the probable departure of ten children from the previous years. We faced a net loss.

I hung around the foyer, practising a welcoming smile. I went to the gate, pretending to collect the mail. A teacher of wisdom (and smiling cynicism) had once told me that the main events in a principal's day were collecting the mail and checking the drains. The drains were okay, so I went and wasted some of Roberta, the secretary's, time. I had one more look up and down the road, then said I needed to go to my office to make some phone calls. In fact, I sat at my desk and had a good cry. Somehow everyone knew, and at morning tea I received sympathetic hugs from some and enquiries about what I thought I was doing wrong from others.

Maybe things would change, maybe there would be the trickle that would lead to a stream, to a river, to a flood. Maybe. When friends, dear friends, who could have sent their children to Newton Central elected to go elsewhere, I was devastated. They were influencers, long before the term was invented, and could have provided the trickle I so desperately wanted, needed. I loved the school and couldn't understand why others didn't. They asked why I expected them to be the ones to risk their children at a school that might have potential but was currently an unknown.

That year *Metro* magazine ran an article about inner-city schools. Newton Central was given a lot of space, and the reporter praised the positive and busy atmosphere she observed. There was a large photo of me looking particularly goofy beside some children's paintings. My words of optimism and idealism were quoted at length, followed by the journalist's summary: 'Unfortunately for Heath, public opinion is unlikely to change.'

For a while 'unfortunately for Heath' became my mantra. There was no option but to accept the situation and just get on with it.

THERE WAS A STRONG compulsion 'to get on with it', not just because this was owed to the kids who were there, but also because this was the dawn of the Tomorrow's School reforms being put together by an enthusiastic prime minister and a successful supermarket magnate. They represented a government which saw virtue in business models, and many of their ideas were based on a book about a school in Tasmania that might have been more successful in print than in reality. Schools were not exactly being told to make money, but clearly they would be lauded if they did. Many of the proposed reforms struck me as excellent; many filled me with apprehension.

I had had a long love–hate relationship with school inspectors. They had always been positive towards me, but I had never felt comfortable at being beholden to them. As well as their role in evaluating individual teachers, they had the responsibility for a collection of schools. In this role they had particular value, especially if their association with a school covered a number of years and they had the opportunity to have come to an informed understanding of a community, its strengths and weaknesses. The inspector allocated to Newton Central had this knowledge. She knew the architectural challenges of some of the rooms, the history of disputes, and the fact that the Ministry of Works did not care about the noise their motorway made. She was a friend, a mentor, a confidante and a person able to smilingly guide me away from more radical ideas. I did not like the idea of her being taken away and replaced with an Education Review Office (ERO), which, from when it was first mooted, seemed to be constructed of checklists, graphs and clipboards – all the usual weaponry of a supermarket stocktake!

I went to numerous meetings about the proposed changes. Of the millions of words uttered at these meetings, two sets still stand out. The first was from a parent from a wealthy suburb who saw himself as a potential board member. 'The first thing I'll do,' he told me, 'is to install a bloody time clock and make those teachers accountable!' I thought of the teachers who left early with a box full of planning and marking that they did at home once family had been fed and husband's shirts ironed; of the deputy principal I would try to encourage to go home because it was 8 p.m. on a Friday night; and the young teachers who would sacrifice most of what young people should be doing so that they could better cater for the needs of the children in their classrooms.

The second memorable quote was from none other than Prime Minister and Minister of Education David Lange, a hero in so many other areas. In his 2005 autobiography, *David Lange: My Life*, he described his vision for education as outlined in a report written by Brian Picot, the grocer he had charged with the task of reforming New Zealand Schools: 'The Picot Report proposed a model of administration which was based on local control. Above all it was a democratic model, aimed at harnessing the most powerful force in education – the desire of parents to see their children do well at school.'

I was, of course, enthusiastic about this idea as it was expressed at the time, but had some misgivings. At a principals' meeting addressed by David Lange and Brian Picot, I summoned up the courage to ask a question, fearful that my flimsy coracle would not stand up well against the PM's Spanish galleon. I spoke of how I feared that the issue of property management would be the downfall of schools in poorer communities; of how some boards of trustees would have among their parent group architects and engineers willing to take on this responsibility, backed by their knowledge, skill and office resources, while other schools would be lucky to find a builder's labourer to take on this role. The equity and buying power of the maintenance divisions of the current Education Boards would be lost, and many schools would suffer. The prime minister drew a deep breath, unfurled an extra sail (a sail that definitely didn't have 'socialism' written on it) and bellowed, 'You always find some who lack the courage to play the game!'

I sank without a trace.

Tomorrow's Schools was duly introduced. Hundreds of bureaucrats lost their jobs and hundreds of parents struggled to fill the gaps, to learn the new language and how to tick the new boxes. The administrative load on principals increased. Some people relished the new responsibilities and handled them well. They became happy managers and their schools became models of self-management. They had daunting amounts of paperwork covering every aspect of school life, including, in one case, details of the school policy on the correct way to peel oranges. I couldn't bring myself to do it.

The good people of the ERO came to visit, and we had a wonderful time. They seemed to understand what I was trying to achieve. They were excited by the learning they saw, and stated that the school was a safe and stimulating place for children. Their parting words, both verbal and written, oozed positivity but contained an ominous warning: 'The school's challenge is to now record the excellence we observed in written form.' I never saw the point and never wrote the policies and procedures they wanted documented — if the cake tastes okay, why run round with copies of the recipe? I saw my colleagues producing excellent recipes but not baking any cakes. The great liberal reforms, which contained so much that was excellent and optimistic, were becoming buried in bureaucratic demands.

I found myself spending more and more time at school, arriving early and working on Sunday mornings. The Sunday mornings were initially a great uninterrupted time in which to achieve a degree of efficiency. However, parents and teachers alike realised I was there and would come knocking on the door with the words: 'I thought I would come and chat with you while you weren't busy.'

It was around this time that I thought I would streamline my desk and make myself focus on one task at a time, as wise people had advised me to do. I put all except the immediate papers into a cardboard box and put the box into a cupboard. Unfortunately, consciously or unconsciously, I then forgot about the existence of the box and didn't rediscover it for six months. When I had packed it, all the papers had seemed vitally important. Six months of neglect hadn't made an atom of difference; the sky hadn't fallen and I had not been drowned under a tsunami of complaint from bureaucrats screaming neglect. I tried not to be influenced by this experience.

PART AND PARCEL of the spirit of accountability that wafted up and down the corridors of education was the belief that teachers did not adequately evaluate the work and progress of children. Fundamental to this belief was a demand that a child's attainment should be measured against that of her or his age peers. (As an aside, I hate writing 'her and his' and wish we could adopt a gender-neutral term like 'ia', the Māori pronoun that covers third persons of all varieties. Similarly, there seems so much advantage in the pronoun systems of most of the Pacific in which 'we' can be said at least four different ways, with the ability to specify number as either dual or plural, and indicate whether the hearer is part of the group being considered. In Māori, for example, it is possible to come into a crowded room and say 'We are going to bed', and hearers will immediately know how many people are involved and if they, too, are going to join in.)

Pronouns aside, a spirit of evaluation swept through the educational world and produced a great mass of data and testing so that teachers could answer the dread question: 'How is he/she doing?' The expected answer immediately involved reference to those mythical creatures called 'national norms' – how was Johnny, aged six, doing in relation to other six-year-olds? I wanted to say 'Who cares?', but knew there was a chorus of voices yelling 'We care!' My concern was how Johnny was doing in comparison with what he had managed to do yesterday and the day before. I wanted to have an idea of what he might be able to do and how close he was to achieving it. I wanted to know about his social adjustment, his happiness and whether he stole other kids' lunches.

Whenever I needed to ask a teacher about a child's progress, he or she (ia) would bring a swag of written information but never refer to it. They would speak about the child in variable, tentative terms, talk about good days and bad days, about the snakes and ladders that characterise some children's learning. They would talk about positive things that were not necessarily measurable. They would not talk about age peers in different cities, in different countries.

I remembered my days of classroom teaching when we had to fill in a thin brown foolscap book called 'Register of Progress and Achievement'. For a while it had been popular to fill this book with statistics, so that we knew that on 15 March Johnny scored 15 out of 20 in a spelling test. Great information, but it didn't mean much unless we knew the level of the words and, more significantly, whether he was comfortable using them in his everyday writing. There is not much use being able to spell 'phthisis' if you don't want to write about it. The popularity of figures in the P and A Register, as we, its friends, used to call it, was replaced by an enthusiasm for words. One principal had waved my word-filled document around at a staff meeting as a fine example of P and A Register construction. Sadly, he hadn't realised that I had tired of writing inane comments and had filled most of the available space with lines from nursery rhymes.

I know that much of this is cynical and smart, possibly even dishonest, but I do want to highlight the difficulty of reporting on a child's progress in a worthwhile way. To me, there needs to be the occasional dip into comparison with others, but the bulk of information must relate to the child in question. And this is not a task of simple measurement that will lend itself to graphs and glib statements in Parliament. Knowing where a child is at, and what he or she needs next, is a far more complex task than this. It is at the very heart of the art of teaching. I grieve that teachers have allowed this part of their art to be stolen from them by the bean counters.

At this time I resolved that I wanted to restructure the school in a way that would get us away from the dreaded reliance on chronological age. The only way to do this, I believed, was to make each classroom resemble Papuni School, with kids of all ages bundled in together. I knew I had to sell this idea to the staff – not just sell it, but enlist their help to develop it into a workable form.

'Sell' is, of course, the wrong word. What I was looking for was more like conversion and belief. This resulted in a series of long and intense staff meetings. I found these meetings exciting. Most teachers responded with a creativity and commitment that seemed way beyond what I was entitled to expect, given that what I was trying to implement would involve them in lots of extra work. However, I have to report that after one such meeting, a teacher beset with family responsibilities and not wanting to be further burdened by the proposed changes looked at me with anger and, with her lips quivering, hissed, 'We only have consensus decision-making here because that's the way you want it!'

Sunk again.

16.

I WON THE hearts and minds of some of the teachers. Others expressed reservations but were willing to give it a go. The teacher who still hadn't forgiven me for knocking the Friday afternoon videos on the head said she would do it if she had to. The next task was to communicate the intention to adopt a radical new structure to the parent community.

I wrote a full and detailed outline of the proposal in the fourth paragraph of an overly long school newsletter. Yes, I did know most people seldom read beyond paragraph two. They would look for their child's name and, sometimes, for a list of upcoming events.

One couple, one of the few Pākehā to send their child to the school, and then only because of its convenient location to their work, made an appointment to see me. I braced myself for their reaction, but was still surprised by its vehemence. They were angry and distressed. For them, the proposed changes meant the school would no longer look like the places they had been to as children, and this amounted to a heresy. The father lost his cool and shouted. I lost my cool and shouted. The mother called us 'boys' and calmed us down. She didn't give us lollies.

We talked for a long time. They spoke of how they expected more consideration, given that they represented the minority group I so desperately needed in the school. This made me feel like shouting again. I wrote them letters of explanation and finally won some grudging acceptance. But they also made me see that the struggling immigrant community of Newton Central was too busy trying to survive to have the luxury of questioning teachers. We were supposed to know what we were doing. Had I been teaching in a middle-class suburb, my attempt to throw out a traditional model of education would never have floated — it would have been blasted to bits before it even left the slipway.

In 1990 we launched into it. A lot of time was spent making up class lists that would give a balance in number, gender, ethnicity and ability. Families were given the option of their children all being in the same room or different rooms. Almost all chose the first option, which was great considering we called the system 'family grouping'. For the next six years this was how we operated. Systems were refined, community acceptance increased and the school roll began to reflect the demography of the neighbourhood. In fact, we had a steady flow of people from outside the area electing to come to us.

By 1996, however, things started to fall apart, largely because of staff changes. The original group of teachers who had accepted the idea and worked on its development, responded to its challenges and enjoyed seeing it working, underwent change. Some left, but, more significantly, the growth of the roll meant that new teachers joined us. Most found the day-to-day work in a multi-level classroom too much of a shock. They had known about it, had much of it explained, but were bowled over by the reality — the cold shower in the tropics syndrome. In fairness, I have to acknowledge that it is much easier to accept something new if you have been part of its creation than it is to try to fit yourself into someone else's creation.

In the years in which family grouping had its heyday there were, I believe, a number of real advantages for children. Let me do the good teacher thing and present these advantages as a list:

1. In broad terms, ideas about chronological age became less important than ability and attainment levels. If I asked a teacher who in the room was eight years old, he or she would answer this less readily than a question about who was at a particular reading level. We came to believe that if you had a classroom of children of the same age, the spread of ability and attainment would be from X to Y. If you had children aged five to eleven, the range of ability and attainment would probably still be X to Y.

2. A child could stay with the same teacher for more than one year, and in fact some children ended up having their entire primary school education with the one teacher. This gave child and teacher the chance to develop a deep and close knowledge of each other. I told parents

218

they could change to a different teacher whenever they wanted to, but this option was seldom taken up. People argue that this deprived children of the strengths that can come from variety. There is truth in this, but I believe we are talking about a very close relationship, akin to the relationship children have with their parents — a relationship where the values of stability and consistency far outweigh other considerations. We called this family grouping because we wanted what we were developing to have the characteristics of the best of families, and consistency was high on this list of characteristics.

3. The beginning of each new year did not bring the usual kerfuffle as a teacher got to know a new group of children, established rules and routines, and learned about levels and needs. This was already known and in place, as were children's friendships and their knowledge of where the reading books and paintbrushes were kept. I would walk around the school at five past nine on the morning of the first day of a new year and be overjoyed, overwhelmed really, by the fact that it was as if we had not been away for six weeks. Everything slotted back into place, wheels turned again, and the whole place just felt busy. It was a delight to be there, and to be spending time in classrooms with such a wonderful and courageous group of teachers — time I probably should have spent in my office, writing it all up for the Review Office before the sin of simply enjoying the cake came back to haunt me.

4. One of the constant challenges in a conventionally organised school is balancing numbers. If you have significantly more children in Standard Two than, for example, in Standard Three, do you just make the classes at one level bigger than at the other, or do you contemplate dreaded composite classes? We were able to keep numbers evenly balanced — anyone could go anywhere.

THERE WERE THREE further significant advantages that I want to outline more fully later. The first concerns new-entrant children, the second Māori language education, and the third involves care of children with special needs. But first I will tell you the story of one student, a true story that may illustrate what could sometimes happen in a family-grouped classroom at Newton Central School.

Wednesday was often a day when the unexpected occurred. Monday had its beginning-of-the week turmoil and Tuesday was the day to sort out Monday's unfinished business. Wednesday allowed me to look up, have a bit of a think. I always had a sense of anticipation about what Wednesday might bring.

On this particular Wednesday it brought Frankie. Or, more accurately, he brought himself. I had never seen him before. He charged into my office and flung himself into one of the steel-framed, vinyl-covered chairs that I had arranged in a small circle for cosy chats with parents — the new, the anxious, the pleased and the displeased. These ugly, standard-issue chairs were low, with sloping backs and wooden arms.

They were surprisingly comfortable, so much better for a chat than the one-on-each-side-of-a-big-desk arrangement that so many of my colleagues seemed to favour.

Frankie let his shoulders slip halfway down the back, his bottom balanced on the front edge of the seat, legs splayed out in front of him. It was a gunslinger pose, full of feigned casualness, indifference, insolence, defence and flight-readiness.

'Good morning,' I said. 'I am Tim.'

He lifted his head slightly, raised an eyebrow, and assessed how dangerous I might be.

Again, long-ingrained first responses played out in my mind – Sit up, better still, stand when you speak to me, shoulders back, speak when you are spoken to, knock before you enter, look me in the eye, call me Sir – I could have sent him into flight so easily. Instead, I waited, but came to sense he was better at waiting than I was.

He looked to be about ten. He was lean, wiry, his leanness emphasised by pants that were a bit too big and a shirt that was a bit too small. His hair reminded me of thistles in the back paddock, unrestrained and unattended. There was a lopsided muscular arrangement about his mouth that allowed him to pull one side down while the other was raised in a sneer. The scar on his right cheek was in the shape of a tick, but I don't think it was there as a sign of approval. He didn't speak or smile, his mouth clamped shut. It was an act, copied from heaven knows who, that said 'I don't like you and you can't hurt me.' If I did, or said, the wrong thing, he would pull out his six-gun and shoot me. So, we waited.

Suzie, the school secretary, bustled in with some papers. She smiled at him – smiled the smile that was one of the reasons I employed her. A smile as big and reassuring as summertime. A smile that reached out and embraced him in a way he might not have been embraced before.

'You gonna come to our school?' she asked. 'Hope so,' she added with another smile and a chuckle.

He had no show.

'They tol' me to come here. Tol' me to get enrolled.'

'Where were you before?' I thought I had to contribute something.

'That stink school.'

'And the name of that stink school . . . ?'

Fortunately, Suzie took over, and he told her the school's name.

'And what about you, sweetheart, what do we call you? Do we call you "stink boy" or you got another name?'

'Frankie, I'm Frankie.'

He looked at Suzie and they both grinned.

Suzie could do this, and it was funny, friendly, and warm enough to get him talking. She had told me lots over the years, and I knew that she, too, had been raised in Frankie Land.

I left them talking: she armed with clipboard, enrolment form, smile and pen, he disarmed. I rang the previous school. I had been to teachers' college with the principal. Even back then she had specialised in never calling a spade a manually operated digging implement. It was a bloody spade, and it, like the rest of the world, was either black or white. She had been marked out early as having leadership potential, and she did, in a bulldozer in a barnyard kind of way. She thought I was a 'woolly woofter', hamstrung by inefficient liberalism, something she mentioned whenever we were at meetings together.

'Frankie!' she bellowed down the phone. 'You are welcome to the little bugger. He'll climb the walls and make most teachers do the same. He'll swear and perform and generally be a pain in the arse. I reckon he'll be running your school by lunchtime. And he can't bloody read. I never bothered to find out which prison his parents are in. Guess they'll wait till he joins them. Good luck, mate.'

She laughed.

Suzie's laughter was a summer evening breeze, but my fellow principal's was a winter wind from the south. She was too busy to give me further details, and I was referred to a secretary who seemed to think she was working for the Governor-General. I was given a series of facts — damage, fights, suspensions, more damage, reading age or lack of it, a total of thirteen different schools, Social Welfare involvement.

I went back to my office where Suzie and Frankie were having a picnic which seemed to involve her lunch and my banana.

'Okay, Frankie, my man, we can take you to your new classroom now,' I beamed, undoing all Suzie's good work in an instant.

'I think you should be in April's class,' Suzie said, treating his flight to the door as an invitation to give him a hug.

I started to tell Suzie I was the principal and I was the one to decide which class he should go to.

'Yes, Sir,' she said, 'but you know April's the best one for him, and I've just saved you from agonising over whether you should put him there or keep space for a demanding parent who has heard a rumour about the wonders of our lovely April and how it would be an injustice not to move their already indulged darling into her room.'

I held up my hand to signal her to stop, a gesture she took to mean surrender.

As I've said, one of the virtues of family grouping is that children of any age can go into any room. This has the advantage, among other things, of allowing class sizes to be kept about the same. April's class was getting bigger than all the others.

April called her children together. I say 'call', but it was more of a quietly spoken request – children listen when adults make their rare commands sound like requests. If April's soft request had been to climb the outside of the Sky Tower, they would have done that, too.

'This is Frankie. He is going to be part of our family. Please welcome him.'

The children made welcoming noises in their home languages. A babble, but a warm babble.

Frankie seemed as if he was struggling to feel unwelcome. He kept glancing at April, then looking away. I think he instantly liked her but was afraid she might turn out to be a schoolteacher.

Without being told to, the children went back to the variety of different tasks they had been involved in. It all seemed natural and easy, but it was underpinned by April's hours of preparation, her knowledge of what each child needed and the attitudes to learning that she had been able to build. For most of the kids this was their third year with her – they knew the expectations, the patterns and the rewards.

Frankie stood there. Megan, aged five, came up to him, her right foot extended. He looked puzzled.

'Shoelace,' she said, with an air of patience. 'Shoelace undone.'

Frankie went down on one knee and tied the shoelace.

It wasn't all perfect after that. There were meltdowns and misunderstandings, defiance of other teachers and days of unexplained absence, but in the classroom he seemed to feel safe. It would be easy to say he felt at home, but I don't think home and safety went together for Frankie.

He became April's right-hand man, in charge of shoelaces. He had an unexpected flair for tidying up. After a few weeks, I asked her about his academic progress. She smiled, of course, and spoke of how he seemed to want to learn and how he was self-conscious about the gaps in his knowledge. She said he sometimes attached himself to a group of much younger children. She thought he might be doing this to pick up learning he had missed. When he was putting books away, he would pause for increasingly long periods, looking through them, even asking others about some of the words. He loved listening to stories. She said he never managed to call her April, as everyone else did. She was always 'Miss', while I, clearly a lesser being, was always Tim.

No school is free from bullying. There is a casual cruelty about children and a human desire to peck our way to the top. I like to think I worked hard to keep these things in check, and found one of the best ways was to station adult observers around the playground, parents who could become almost unseen, able to watch what was really happening and, we hoped, help us change undesirable behaviour. Frankie had a more direct approach — he made it clear that if anyone hurt a kid from his room, he would kill them.

About nine o'clock on a Wednesday morning about eight months later, I had a phone call from a school in a rural town about three hundred kilometres away. The caller told me a boy had just arrived, untidy and surly, his hair all over the place. He had flopped into a chair and was not speaking. They had looked through his bag and found a book with the name of our school.

'Do you know him?' the caller asked. 'I mean how do you deal with a ratbag like this? Last thing we need. Like we are a really settled school, long-term families, if you know what I mean.'

'Sounds like my friend Frankie,' I said, fearing this would be interpreted as sarcasm.

'Jeez, hang on, he's just pulled down a few things off the wall and bolted through the door. Nah, the DP's got him by the collar, should be okay. Just send his records, will you, and we'll do our best to straighten him out.'

How was I going to tell April?

How was she going to tell her children?

Who was going to tie up shoelaces?

17.

I HAD, FOR many years, worried about the typical new entrants' room. In most schools this room would start the year with three or four children. This number would grow as children in the community progressively turned five. I also worried, of course, about five being regarded as a good age to start school: 'You are five, my son, off to school you go, ready or not!' Most sons were not ready. Class numbers would grow and the teacher would become concerned about how many children she could handle. Here I have to say I never met a male new- entrant teacher and, almost without exception, new-entrant teachers are marvellous, warm, caring, skilful women. I do not have any criticism of them – well, most of them – just of the structures within which they work.

The busy new entrants' room, as numbers grow, becomes a bustling place where survival of the fittest prevails. Those ready and able, those for whom the environment has some cultural familiarity, those with strong language skills, do well. In a small, significant but neglected study, New Zealand's Professor Marie

Clay had her research students observe in new entrants' classrooms. Their main task was to record interactions which resulted in children responding by saying additional things. Clay saw these 'talk more' responses as vital not just to a child's language development, but also to their understanding that the classroom was a place that had something to offer.

Children want to talk more, as can be so easily demonstrated: if you ask a typical group of five-year-olds a question, they will wave their hands in an enthusiasm to answer matched only by that of young birds who see their parents returning to the nest with a fat worm or two. Most children, that is. For others, the environment is overwhelming, was overwhelming from the start. They are the ones who sit quietly in the corners with their heads down, fiddling with blocks, not books, and, significantly, not having any 'talk more' engagements with the teacher — with anybody, for that matter. And, as you will have guessed, these children are disproportionately Māori and Pasifika, the very ones who need so much before the school experience can become warm and safe. We have a system, a structure, that serves to compound their disadvantage, not overcome it.

Language development and readiness to read go hand in hand. It seems like an oversimplification, but human beings can't get meaning from reading if they don't understand the words and the word usage they are reading. It is true that once we have the decoding skills, we can read words in unknown languages. I can read passages in French reasonably well, but, because little of what I read coincides with known vocabulary, very little contains any sense. The child struggling with English needs language experiences, not reading experiences, needs to be somewhere which encourages him or her to talk more, needs to know that a feke and an octopus are one and the same creature.

It is not, of course, just the children for whom English is a second language who face these obstacles; it is also the many who come to school with limited language experiences in any language. It can be argued that if language is the tool of concept development, then the child with a strong first language will do well in a second language – many millions of multilingual children living in European countries are testimony to this contention. We have, however, many children who arrive at school without the gift of language richness in their school bags. Their school bags probably don't have lunch in them either. Their parents, or parent, because of stress, poverty, tension, alcohol, disillusion, or having been dumped on themselves by an alien school system, have been unable to provide this gift. These children come into the bright light and clamour of a new entrants' room unable to cope. They become, usually, the quiet ones who are much in need of being noticed but desperate not to be. Or, if they still have a bit more spirit, they become Frankies or something even more exciting.

With the best will in the world, with hearts full of aroha and heads full of experience, it is simply not possible for the teacher to sit with these children and talk with them, to spend the hours of one-to-one time that is needed. However, this becomes so much more possible in the family-grouped classroom. Firstly, there are only a few new entrants in each room – the maximum I recall is three. Secondly, there are other mature speakers in the room, older children who can converse about simple things, like where to hang your coat, and more complex stuff, like why Humpty Dumpty found it necessary to sit on a wall. There are Frankies to discuss shoelaces, and, when there is the happy circumstance of an older sibling, there is someone to discuss where the shoes had been left after they were taken off.

Older siblings tended to prepare the way for their five-year-olds. There would be talk of birthdays, their dates and how they were celebrated. They would arrive and present the brother or sister to the class with pride and excitement. Some of this was a bit 'look at me and my cute little pet', but all of it made starting school a warm swim and not an unwilling plunge into cold and dangerous waters.

I believe that in every society it is seen as desirable for older siblings to care for younger ones. Māori speak of the tuakana-teina relationship in this regard; in Sāmoa the looking after of a younger sibling is a formalised responsibility. In villages you can see children, usually girls, sometimes as young as seven or eight, lugging around 'their' four-year-old charge, and at times being punished for the younger child's transgressions.

It is true that in the early years family grouping at Newton Central thrived because for many Māori and Pasifika kids this kind of caring seemed an easy and natural thing to do. It is also true that in later years I had complaints from Pākehā parents who had enjoyed the caring their children had received when they were five or six, but who, now their children were older, did not want to see perceived educational opportunities impaired by having to look after younger children. Hallelujah! Hallelujah! Hallelujah! Hallelujah!!!

No, I didn't undertake studies with identical twins, one with me, the other in a traditional new entrants' room, and the whole sample of children involved was probably not statistically significant, perhaps less than one hundred, but I am sure children starting school this way had a happier experience. It does not seem logical to expect children to learn in a place where they are fundamentally unhappy, and yet this has been the experience of so many. If Charles Dickens' portrayal of schools in his day is correct, it would seem that creating misery was the fundamental aim of the educationalists. I wanted children to be happy and I wanted them to learn from each other. I am sure that for those with particular skills and aptitudes, the example of the older children served to enhance these. This seemed particularly true in art and sports.

AS I WRITE THIS I feel other educational hobby horses champing at the bit, desperate to be allowed a gallop. This is as good a time as any to release one of these − the 'teaching' of painting and drawing. There is, I believe, in every child an innate desire to make pictures, to create a visual image. Children want to take a crayon and a piece of paper, or a convenient wall or a pristine white dress, and make marks. These marks, the way they are arranged, the way the colours combine, their size and accuracy, are made without inhibition or self-consciousness.

Then we start to teach them, show them the right way. We hold up someone else's picture and say, 'This is really good. Well done, Mary, you worked hard. Everyone, try to be like Mary.' And everyone tries to be like Mary, their own creativity shrivelling as they do so. And we give them those abominations called colouring books. Colouring books are okay for an adult who can't afford proper therapy, but they serve to show kids that there are drawing skills and that they shouldn't attempt anything until their drawing skills are up to standard. Colouring books teach children that art is a quiet, gentle activity that lulls, that fills in time; it is definitely not something wild, noisy and visceral that excites. And if you give your child a paint-by-numbers book, you might as well make it overt and chain him in a colourless dungeon until he relinquishes every gram of his natural creativity.

Adults have a responsibility to show children new media and tools they can use, and to supply some ideas about what they might make. And that's about it, apart from cleaning up. So often, when I conducted an art session with children, I found myself working hard to dare them to be children, to rediscover who they were before people came along and showed them 'the right way'. In my ideal classroom, the old run-down prefab out the back, there would be art supplies always at the ready and children able to use them when they felt like it. The whole emphasis would be on process, not results, which means of course that the results are sometimes splendid. In an art display we had a painting of the Auckland Harbour Bridge by Jonathan Putu, then aged five. If it had been an auction, I suspect I could have sold this memorable picture to other parents for hundreds of dollars. And of course I want to say it's not about money – but I have galloped far enough on this one.

If young children benefited from the example of older ones in most subject areas, they certainly also benefited in physical activities. Not rocket science: you learned to run faster so you could keep up; you learned to catch so you would be in the team; you learned to try hard because you were aware there were higher standards to be achieved.

I loved watching new entrants at Newton Central. I loved seeing them happy and, more than that, talking their heads off, and demanding new books and well-tied shoelaces.

18.

I CAN HEAR YOU, Dear Reader, doubly Dear Reader if you are the parent of a young child, thinking that all this happiness, all these caring big kids and all this messy artwork is all very fine, but what about the essentials like learning to read and write, to add and subtract and to salute the flag? The last one is easy – we never did it, and I tended to fly children's artwork from the flagpole anyway.

I don't want to be glib or to say things I can't prove, but I want to outline more of my beliefs about children learning to read, even though I know I risk doing that primary school teacher thing of saying something yet again, just to make sure you get it.

Firstly, and perhaps most importantly, children must be ready. They must have had enough time talking and listening; they must have discovered the value of stories; they must have had time, just as I had, for something in their brains to be mature enough to allow the dots and the squiggles to be joined and achieve consistency and meaning. This often doesn't happen, or can't happen, until children are older than five — and I should really have said boys, not children. So often I would ask teachers and parents to wait. It will happen when he is ready, I'd tell them: we don't all like broccoli when it is first put on our plates, but this doesn't necessarily mean we won't eat mountains of it later in life. If we wait, we avoid making a child feel pressured, inadequate and somehow so lacking in whatever it is they are meant to have that they need to be extracted from class for special attention.

Here I know I will run into direct conflict with the good people, the excellent people, who run reading recovery programmes. I never felt comfortable with this programme. It is based on children being selected by the results of a test called 'The Six Year Net' — like all nets, it catches some of its target species, those ready for a little nudge, but there is always a large 'by-catch' of those not ready for the painstaking help that seems to characterise reading recovery. It would, I think, be fine if they didn't go fishing until kids turned seven.

In the 1960s there was a great debate in linguistics. On the one side, the American structuralist linguist Leonard Bloomfield and his allies maintained that external structures not only could be placed on a language, but needed to be placed if it were to be properly analysed. This idea goes back a long way. William Williams's 1844 publication *A Dictionary of the New Zealand Language and a Concise Grammar*, for example, seemed to want to use the Latin grammatical model for te reo Māori. On the other side, Noam Chomsky famously postulated 'the structure is in the data'. There is something liberating about this stance in that it honours indigenous languages by recognising their independence and integrity — they do not need to be hung on a Western model to make sense, any more than English, or te reo Māori, needed to hang on a Latin model.

Reading is the same, in that the model that allows someone to read is not the same in every head. There is not one way. I cannot teach you the 'rules' of reading, but I can give you a variety of experiences that will enable you to develop your own set of rules. Somewhere in my head there is a conglomeration of wires, railway lines, switches, words my mother repeated, and instructions written on small sticky pieces of paper, all of which combine to tell me how to read. Your set is different, and a five-year-old's is very different. How good we were, patient and full of praise, when that five-year-old learned how to talk. I so wish we were able to do the same with kids learning how to read, finding their own structure in the data.

Let me further antagonise reading purists. I think everything we use may be able to help in the magical transition from non-reading to reading, but I seriously doubt that teaching phonics is the secret in crossing from one side to the other. In my experience, the people who are best at phonics, and so many other reading exercises, are those who can already read! I recall being told to repeat the sound 'puh' endlessly, and having no reason to believe that it related in any way to the letter 'P' on the page. It seemed yet another example of the madness that beset my volatile teacher. Once I could read, I could issue as many 'puhs' as people wanted and would even walk down the street gifting them to passersby.

So what is my advice to confused and frustrated parents?

The first thing is not to be in a hurry. Your child doesn't have to be the first kid on the street/in the whānau/in your work group to learn to read. Don't be one of those people who somehow browbeat their child into making a meaningless response to the letters of the alphabet. It doesn't mean a damn thing and will probably put them off. 'Barking at print', we call it in the trade. How your child reads at six, or even seven, doesn't matter nearly as much as how they read at twenty-six or twenty-seven.

Don't let it be too much of a big deal. I have known kids who seem to believe whether they are loved or not loved depends on whether they can read. Makes it a bit of tightrope act, doesn't it?

And, with full knowledge that I am being repetitive, remember how good you were when they were learning to talk, and try to be the same. The mispronounced word seemed so cute, whereas the misread word is deemed a dreadful thing. The positive thing to do is to expose your child to books at a young age. I know a truly brilliant young mum who asked those wanting to bring gifts for the new baby not to bring clothes, or knitted hats, or gold or frankincense or myrrh, but to bring books. She and her baby have a huge collection, which she started reading out loud prenatally. Read books and talk about them. Let the child know you hold books in high esteem.

Look for signs about how healthy and okay your child is. Can he or she sit still and listen to a story? Can they retell the story? Can they tell you long, complicated stuff about anything, no matter how trivial or boring it may seem to you? Can they play with others? Can they play for an extended period of time? Can they catch a ball, stand on one leg, climb up onto the couch, pick up a small block? Does their hearing seem okay? Do they learn routines and the major no-nos to do with safety? If all this seems okay, then they will most probably learn to read when they are ready. If, however, you observe possible physical problems with eyes, ears, balance, coordination and stamina, then it is best to get this checked by an appropriate medical person, the sooner the better. So many kids don't learn to read not because they don't have the ability to do so, but because their ears have been gunked up for years and they can't bloody hear.

Sadly, there are some children who have experienced all of the right things but still find that reading eludes them. These are the few who have genuine dyslexia, a condition I do not believe is as common as some parents would have had me believe. Reading doesn't click into place for these children, and they do need the expert services of people like reading recovery teachers. In some cases an early diagnosis can and should lead to early help, but for the majority, just keep reading to them and quietly hoping.

Young children at Newton Central had an older reading buddy. These buddies had undergone some training, and most were intuitively wonderful – patient, enthusiastic and genuinely involved in the reading process. All said they learned a lot themselves. I like to think our early readers were listened to three or four times a day.

We did not turn everyone into a competent and relaxed reader, but I like to think we came close. It is my fervent hope that there are very few ex-Newton Central students among the ranks of the non-readers who end up unhappy, disillusioned and, all too often, in jail.

I HAVE ALWAYS BELIEVED that physical activity is essential for growing children. And for grown children. For all their brilliance and dedication in every other area, the teachers at Newton Central never fully agreed with me. Their physical education programmes were tokens, and their swimming programmes were worse. In fairness, they pleaded lack of time — as experts and politicians piled more and more into the curriculum, subjects that many regarded as trivial or frivolous, like art, music and physical education, became more and more marginalised. With the exception of the young women who came to school in track pants and running shoes, most teachers saw little to lure them and their children into the great outdoors.

I organised some sports afternoons, but this was no substitute for daily exercise, let alone thrice-daily exercise. I found, after a few years, that I preferred to spend lunchtimes outside, away from the complaints, frustrations and bloody-minded whinges being expressed in the staffroom. This was often my best way to get to know some of the children and get a feel for the health of the playground. I would organise games, especially cricket. At the time I was still playing club cricket and, without being too English public school about it, deeply believed that cricket was an excellent way to develop character — where else do you get disappointment, boredom, intermittent danger, extraordinary usage of time, peer criticism and just enough success to sustain interest in such a neat package?

Shariful, a ten-year-old boy from Bangladesh, joined the school. He was quiet, seemed depressed and was socially isolated. In one of my lunchtime wanders I found him sitting under a tree, head in hands, not weeping but clearly thinking about it. I asked him to walk with me. His English was limited, and he was reluctant to talk. However, he sparked up a bit when I mentioned cricket — I think the Bangladeshi team was visiting New Zealand at the time. I suggested we join the game I knew was happening on our small inadequate field. (How can you run a sports programme without adequate space?)

His face showed that classic dilemma of wanting to but not wanting to reveal how much he wanted to. He said he liked to bowl, so we shouldered our way into the game and I organised the ball into his hand, depriving a kid who had probably waited all lunchtime to get his turn. Shariful strode to the beginning of what was an overly long run and started charging in. I was fearful that when he got to the wicket, he would deliver a hopeless and slow wide, but no, in the best *Boys' Own* tradition, he delivered a rocket — more accurate than anything we had seen, and so fast it made our ground seem smaller and even more inadequate. The ball reared up and fizzed past the batsman's head. He was from a church-going home, but he was still a ten-year-old boy and this enabled him to yell 'Shitting Jesus!' and other expressions of admiration. With one ball, everybody wanted to be Shariful's friend, and a smile never left his face.

I recruited him for the kids' team I ran on Saturday mornings at the Grafton Cricket Club. Everyone who saw him marvelled at his ability but said his run-up was too long. I did a special home visit to enlist the support of his father and his uncles to get him to shorten his run. They thought I was mad and switched the conversation to schoolwork.

I played for the Grafton Cricket Club's President's Grade Eleven for many years. Our wicket keeper was a courier driver. He maintained that one day, as he drove onto the North-Western motorway ramp from Newton Road, he looked over at the school grounds and saw me bowl one of my leg breaks, a ball that I had mastered, albeit with an action reminiscent of a pūkeko with an injured wing. He said he laughed so much he nearly crashed. He also said he wished he had been a teacher.

KIDS NEED TO RUN, jump, wrestle and climb. They also need to sing, to dance and to make music. I employed my friend Linda, from Waiuku days, to be a music specialist. She, influenced by the teachings of composer Carl Orff, ran music sessions in which every child seemed enthusiastic and involved. They made music, learned of the joy and discipline of music. I loved to listen and observe these sessions. I wonder if I had spent this time writing words for the ERO, as I was told I should have, would I now look back on these experiences and smile in the same way?

Every year, in the depths of winter when there had been consistent rain for a few days, I had childish joy organising the Great Annual Mud Day. This very simple event involved taking groups of city kids outside to play in the mud and the rain. It was one of the few privileges reserved exclusively for Year Six students in their final year at Newton. Several days before, I would send a letter home with the kids, telling parents what was involved and seeking their permission for their child to participate. Parents and children had to agree to the following conditions: bring a complete set of mud clothes, a fresh pair of knickers, a towel and something warm to change into. In addition, agree that the child can be hosed down with cold water afterwards. This was the only time, ever, I sent a letter home to be signed and received 100 per cent back, all properly signed, every item accounted for.

I would don my gumboots and parka — the full Papuni hunting outfit — and march onto the field with a group of twittering children, giggly, hugging themselves, clasping nervous hands in front of them, looking for the biggest puddle. Once the initial hesitant slide was done, their inner mudlark was unleashed and they were away. They would slide down the bank, dive headlong into puddles, throw mud, and play a form of rugby that resembled the rules only in the choice of ball. The girls would shriek and the boys make trumpeting noises. They would lie on their backs and gaze, open-mouthed, at the rain. They would wrestle in ankle-deep muddy water. And all the time they would grin and laugh, even when they were hit with the pain of an extra-long slide or an accurately thrown mudball. In short, they had fun.

Perhaps the sense of fun diminished a bit when the cold hose was turned on them, but the noise levels didn't. When it was all over and they were in dry, warm clothes, hair wet but neatly combed, the group would become companionably quiet. There was a sense of achievement, something I hoped they would be able to tell their families about around the dinner table or, at least, during the TV advertisements.

In the winter months I would hold lunchtime soccer games in the hall for the older children. This would involve teams of five-a-side and a foam-rubber ball. Of all the sports activities I involved myself in, none had the same level of dare-devil intensity. Ten-year-olds threw themselves into these games with more recklessness than First Fifteen rugby players. I don't know whether it was because the weather had cooped them up inside for too long or whether their desire to beat their peers was far stronger than I had realised, but the games were a frenetic mixture of running, sliding, diving and crashing. Huge fun and not too many injuries, all things considered.

Not every 'special' activity worked. Each term I held an exclusive lunch, in my office, for children who wore glasses. There would be fish and chips and unhealthy drinks. We would discuss glasses and how they helped us — not as much fun as sliding in the mud, but I think helpful for the children involved. I would, however, get phone calls from some other parents whose children suddenly started complaining of bad eyesight and demanding glasses.

THERE WERE SERIOUS things to do, like teaching maths. My own career as a mathematician was characterised by lack of ability, concentration and perseverance. My teachers were more kindly than those in Sāmoa, who wrote 'Totally average and totally lazy' on school reports — had they done so, it would have been totally justified. I remember walking into the School Certificate exam room with a friend whose mathematical apathy was possibly even greater than mine; he suggested that we stay for an hour, do what we could and then leave and go for a swim. We did this. I don't remember the swim, but my maths result, 15 per cent, has stayed fixed in my mind and profoundly influenced my approach to maths teaching. I had the advantage of knowing how difficult it could be, and this made me determined to make maths understandable and, if at all possible, fun. True, it is hard to squeeze fun into, or out of, fractions, but I tried.

It is also true that I found it hard to keep up with the latest party line issued by the Ministry. I experienced the wheeling out of at least five versions of New Maths, but came to recognise that maths always seemed to go better for children who knew their tables. (It is interesting that we say 'their tables' — they are universal, but individuals must grasp them and make them their own.)

I believe in the rote learning of tables in part because this is one way of getting something anchored in that ever-moving sea that is the young brain. Of course, it is essential that a child knows and understands what $6 \times 5 = 30$ means. They must be able to get thirty counters and organise them into five sets of six and six sets of five. They have to tell me stories about farmers with thirty sheep and either putting six in five paddocks or five in six paddocks. They may be able to rabbit off $9 \times 4 = 36$, but need to be equally quick to tell me that there are nine groups of four in thirty-six.

Teaching and learning tables became almost a full-time job. At Newton Central School we held tables competitions, for which there would be intense practice. I encouraged parents to recite tables with their kids as they did the dishes together. Children hated this suggestion – not the tables part of it, but the dishes. Each class would find a champion and then we would hold a school-wide final, pitting champion against champion in a ruthless knockout contest in front of a deliriously excited crowd. Eventually we would find a school champion, steely-eyed and totally focused, able to answer tables questions quicker than I could ask them. I trust these winners haven't subsequently gone through life with addled brains, unable to remember anything that lacks a plus or multiplication sign. And, I have to add, by way of a commercial, I suppose, that the class champions were not necessarily the oldest children in the room.

It is my belief that this emphasis on tables gave children a basis on which to make estimations. Given that most calculations in the modern world are made on an electronic device, it seems essential that we build into our brains some way of roughly verifying the answer the machine has given us. We may not know that $654 \times 4 = 2616$, but we have to be able to expect two digits in the region of 24 at the beginning of the answer.

This is, of course, only a snippet of the activities that took place in classrooms, but it is an essential snippet. The question of how an answer was arrived at was the one most frequently asked. The validity of tables, drills and telling the story of an equation may be endorsed by the next New Maths syllabus to be published – who knows?

19.

THE LIFE AND SOUL of a school can either be seen as a complex fabric, woven from many often-disparate threads, or it can be seen as an organisation based on a few simple beliefs. I hope the latter is true and that all the weaving and unpicking arises from these beliefs. If this is the case, then among my paramount beliefs are the following three: the right of every child to be at school, regardless of what their learning needs might be; the need to demonstrate and teach care for the environment; and the provision of opportunities for learning and preserving te reo Māori.

I think that if children with learning difficulties are grouped together with children of similar needs, then the group is likely to operate at the level of the lowest common denominator. I acknowledge that this is a very general statement. I also acknowledge that the range of some children's needs demands the skills of specialised teachers and institutions. The developing of specific skills with deaf or blind children are the obvious examples. However, if it is at all possible for a child to be in a mainstream setting, the influence of other children will raise the expectations of everyone involved, including parents and children. I don't like the term 'mainstreaming' – it somehow reminds me of instructions I was given when I needed a urine test. 'Inclusion' is an okay term, but I do prefer simply 'going to school'. It is such a wonderful thing for the parent of a child with big needs to be able to say 'My child is going to school', to be able to talk about the school, to have a little moan about it as most parents do. I believe that at some level, however severe the disability is, a child gains something from being at school and observing how other children behave, even if they are not able to fully participate.

Stella was eighteen when she first started to spend time at the school. She had been a pupil here in her primary school days and had gone on to have a reasonably successful time at secondary school. After finishing college she had not been able to find a job, and spent her time helping run the family home, looking after her younger siblings and an array of other relatives. She would arrive at school in the mornings, a mother hen with a cluster of chicks at various stages of independence and exuberance. I enjoyed watching her marshal them with a mixture of humour, understanding and a frown that let the more adventurous ones know they were getting close to the boundaries. I don't know what she did when the boundaries were crossed, but I suspect that just the knowledge that she, the princess in their lives, was unhappy was a sufficient tug on the reins.

We had parents at school who had reached much higher levels of education, and who regarded themselves as having in-depth knowledge of children, but who still failed to give their own children the security of established limits. It is, I think, a responsibility of parents and teachers to set boundaries and apply them consistently. Once this is done, the nagging can stop, each situation no longer needs to be debated, and children can feel safe and have fun. Children need to know the limits, just as little Huki needed to know he couldn't play in the mud all the time, just as those I encouraged to play in the mud needed to know the rules before we started. I remember a parent who rang up and said, 'I can't bring him to school. He won't get dressed.' I told her to bring him in his pyjamas, give him the benefit of knowing that actions, or the lack of them, have consequences. Adults need to set the rules, because if we leave it to children we learn all over again the truth of *The Lord of the Flies*.

Stella knew these things from the experience of being part of a large Pasifika family and from her intuitive common sense. At the time, we were looking for teacher aides to help look after the increasing number of children with high-level special needs we were enrolling. This programme was under the leadership of the deputy principal, Greg Roebuck, now principal of New Lynn School. Greg was outstanding in his dedication to special-needs teaching and to his training and organisation of the teacher aides. He approached Stella and asked her if she wanted to become a teacher aide. She protested that she hadn't been all that great at school, she didn't know enough and her skills were meagre. Little did she know we had observed her in action and knew she had the qualities and attitudes we needed, so we bullied her into the job. Of course, she started in a tentative and shy manner, but this was a luxury that quickly disappeared as the immediate demands of the job grabbed her. She had a kid to look after and to integrate into the class as fully as possible. One of the great things about teaching is that you have little time to think about it — the task is in front of you, immediate, restless, waving its hand in the air, demanding attention. Stella plunged into it and became invaluable to the child she was assigned to, to his family, to the class and to the school.

Stella was part of what became an extraordinary team of ten mostly local young women from similar backgrounds. These women were intuitively excellent, were open to Greg's gentle training, and had a patience with their children that can only be called love. They learned to treasure the smallest increments of progress — five seconds of eye contact could become a cause for celebration. I also believe their work as teacher aides demystified school for them, and they came to realise that teachers, with their human shortcomings, were not creatures elevated by some mysterious superiority. They began to see school as a setting in which they could operate confidently and make a contribution. I like to think the school helped them see they had potential way above what their own schooling, and perhaps their families, had led them to believe.

After Stella had worked at the school for five or so years, we told her that she had to become a teacher. She rejected this idea, just as she had rejected the idea of becoming a teacher aide. It is significant that the first rejection had been delivered in a shy and halting manner. She knew us now and the second rejection was more 'Gee, but you don't know what you're talking about.' But we did. We made a path for her to go to teachers' college and insisted she walk down it. She is now a very successful teacher, as are the two other teacher aides who followed her down the same path. I think of them, some twenty-three years later, and smile a slightly teary smile.

The family-grouped classroom is an ideal situation for a special-needs child. Patterns of mutual care are already established and there is no sense that someone is too old or too young to be in the group. They can just fit in. At Newton Primary we lacked many specialised skills, but the child's sense of inclusion had to be balanced against this. We always tried to look upon having a special-needs child in the classroom as an advantage for everyone.

This view was beautifully captured in a comment by an eight-year-old pupil. I was showing some prospective parents around the school. The mother was keen, but clearly the father thought his child was entitled to something way better than a multicultural school which couldn't organise children into their proper age groups. He had inspected the toilets and found them lacking. (Most primary school toilets are lacking by two in the afternoon.) We went into the classroom where Libby was a pupil. Libby was in a wheelchair. She dribbled and waved her arms about. At times she made odd noises. The father turned to eight-year-old Esra, who happened to be showing Libby a book.

'Well,' said the father, 'don't you find it distracting and annoying having something like this in the classroom?'

'Why should I?' said Esra. 'She's just a regular kid.'

Needless to say, this family didn't enrol their child. Equally needless to say, my sense of smug jubilation at the perfection of Esra's answer, and the understanding that underlay it, remains with me today.

I may be guilty of painting too much of a happy picture, lapsing into the easy and tempting rosy glow of nostalgia. There were problems – of course there were problems, just as Pius had told me there would be. There were parents who couldn't understand why we didn't do more, and parents who wanted us to do less. There were distressing times when we had to point out that while we could understand disability this was not a licence for bad behaviour. Teachers became weary of the extra demands placed on them, and I know there were times when acting out my ideals placed great burdens on others. Teacher aides sometimes didn't show up and we couldn't find replacements, nor could we have a very needy child at school unassisted. The times of triumph, of the new word, the eye contact, the absence of tantrums, had to be balanced against the daily grind, the repetition, messes that had to be cleaned up and the absence, so often, of fun. Our teacher aides were young and they, too, wanted to sometimes run, dance and sing with the others, and not be eternally condemned to stumble along at the rear.

Here, I want to pay tribute to the many parents of children with special needs who I have met and worked with over the years. They were, without exception, extraordinary and wonderful people. There is no way that parents with children who meet milestones in the manner expected can really understand the lot of parents whose children don't. Once the initial diagnosis is given, disbelief and denial often follow. I remember one young mum who showed me her newborn baby. She told me he was perfect. His overlarge, uncontrolled, lolling head told me he wasn't. She, like so many others, came to accept the diagnosis and, again like so many others, became a scholar of the condition, a fighter for her child's rights and a person capable of more caring than most of us can sustain. And, like so many others, her relationship with the baby's father broke up under the intolerable strain.

The stamina of these parents is so admirable. As a solo parent I found my children exhausting at times, but I could get relief because they could amuse themselves safely. I was rewarded by their achievements, their growth and by the fun that characterised so much of what we did. They were toilet-trained from a young age. I had the reasonable belief that they would grow up capable of independence, of earning a living and contributing to society. How dare I become exhausted?

THE SCHOOL IS perched at the top of a steep slope beside the North-Western Motorway's Newton Road off-ramp. The sound of cars slowing their motorway speed, then climbing this off-ramp was a constant background to outside activities. In addition, there were doubtless silent, more harmful nasties generated by thousands of passing cars creeping over the fence. This traffic intrusion into everyday life underlined the fact that this was an inner-city school. As I have said, I nagged at various authorities to no avail. There was, however, one major success. We spoke with the Auckland City Council, as it was then known, about the dangers many children faced when crossing Great North Road on the way to school. There was a pedestrian crossing, which we lollipop-monitored morning and afternoon, but children often wanted to cross outside these times. An alarming percentage of cars either failed to see them on the crossing or saw their presence as less significant than the desire to get to work on time. We wanted pedestrian-controlled traffic lights installed. I had an on-site meeting with a traffic engineer who uttered words that I have, ever since, quoted to people who seemed to be missing the point. He said, with the utmost solemnity, and a touch of superiority: 'You must realise, Mr Heath, that we are reluctant to install these lights. To do so is to increase statistics of pedestrian-controlled crossing death and injury.' I suggested to him that the bigger picture might be the death and injury rates crossing the road. He looked at me in the same manner maths teachers had tended to look at me when I was at school. However, the lights were duly installed. There were no deaths or injuries, although many motorists may have been a bit later for work.

There was no similar solution to the motorway noise problem, and I resolved that the only thing to do was to accept the limitations of the situation, accept that neither Council nor the Ministry of Works was going to do anything about it. We just did whatever we could to make the school environment as pleasant as possible. The school buildings, more like large houses than institutional rectangles, cried out for gardens, and I spent time the ERO would have had me doing things with bits of paper planting multicultural beds of roses and hibiscus. Some parents joined in, and soon, especially around the administration building, there was an array of flowers, vigorous, colourful and with that eclectic nature that characterises gardens that depend on donations.

All this was happiness, but the slope towards the motorway was not. It covered at least two thousand square metres, and although it had been grassed it was too steep to play on and had ugly slashes of yellow clay where it had eroded. The bank had been shaped when the school had been rebuilt, and had had a regularity imposed upon it by a bulldozer driver who saw more virtue in straight lines than in the preservation of topsoil. Initially, I thought the best thing to do was to purchase an appropriate ride-on mower so that Leon, the groundsman, could keep it looking a bit less like a neglected and mangy meadow. I asked a number of companies to come and demonstrate the machine they thought would be best suited for this situation. Most came, looked at the slope and went away.

One memorable guy looked at the slope, stated it would be no problem and raced up on his shiny little machine. At the top he waved down at us in triumph and turned to come back down. At this point, his mower transmogrified into a toboggan more obedient to gravity than to his frantic swinging of the steering wheel. The machine executed an asymmetrical 360-degree manoeuvre and arrived, backwards, beside us. Leon, a laconic outback Australian, said, 'Bit steep, d'ya reckon, mate?' The ashen driver loaded the mower back on his trailer and departed, muttering.

Eventually we purchased a large self-propelled mower with a detachable buggy. Leon walked it across the slope, with strict instructions that he would doubtless ignore to let the mower go if it became unruly and save himself. He would hitch up the buggy on the flat areas, and sit on it slightly bent forward, moving at the gentle pace of someone who knew there was little point in hurrying. He told me he often thought of the old drivers of horse-drawn coaches he had seen in his Queensland childhood. We talked a lot, Leon and I. His wife, Amy, also worked at the school, as a cleaner. She was the only person, in the ten years I strutted around the place, to tell me to get stuffed. Leon told me this made us members of the same club.

I enjoyed talking with him, listening to his stories. I think this gave me a touch of the male company that is so often missing in a primary school – that and the fact we talked about practical, tangible things. One afternoon we were sitting on a log, discussing the problem of the bank. He had a habit of leaning forward, elbows on knees, rolling a smoke with casual concentration. He would glance towards me when he came to an important part of a story, or when he thought what I was saying was of dubious value, but basically he would just direct his words at the ground in front of him. One of his stories was about his first experience as a drover.

'We was broke as all hell. Mum'd died and Dad'd buggered off somewhere years back. My big sister, Nell, she looked after us, me and the five younger kids. I wasn't at school no more an' I thought I'd get a job droving. Most of us had a crack at droving. They supplied the horses an' I told them I was eighteen an' could ride. They knew I was lyin' but they needed extra hands. About three days out the boss came to me an' gave me this bloody great revolver, kinda oily and shiny and heavy. "Bloody hell, I doan' want that bloody thing, shit no," I said.'

'"You're a shit useless rider, son. It's three days back and

255

another six weeks to go. If you bloody fall off the bloody horse and break ya' bloody leg, then ya'd better just shoot ya' bloody self 'cos we ain't bloody goin' back!" '

Leon said he clung onto the horse all the way there and all the way back. When he reached Brisbane he reckoned they diddled him with the pay and he ended up with only a few shillings. On the way home he spent it all on a big box of 'them roun' wine biscuits', because he thought they were the best grub around. He said Nell had held her hand out for his wages, and when all he could give her was the round wine biscuits, she punched his arm and then gave him a hug.

I told him the story of Steve teaching me to ride — it seemed a bit pale in comparison.

Leon kept the slope under control but never made it look particularly beautiful. In truth it remained an eyesore, a constant reminder that it would always sabotage my dream of making the school an inner-city oasis.

It was about this time that two students taking a perma-culture course at a technical institute entered my life. They had a major assignment which involved planning and developing a large project in a public place. They had seen the dreaded slope from the other side of the motorway and wondered if I would be interested in a planting programme that would cover it with native bush. I was about fifty at the time but still capable of leaping into things with only enthusiasm and optimism as a parachute. Their request seemed made in heaven. It would solve the problem of the bank, it would give us the opportunity to teach kids that planting trees was something they could and should do, it would build community spirit, it would save the planet and Leon's crook knee . . . I danced around the office, reeling off the advantages, already seeing the trees that would become a focal and defining feature of the school. They grinned and, still grinning, told me that what they visualised would cost thousands of dollars.

'No problem,' I said. 'No problem at all.' The school was broke at the time — we didn't charge 'donations' and we employed too many teacher aides, so, indeed, no problem.

The plan was to restore the lost topsoil. This would be done by covering the slope with old carpets, hundreds of them, and then covering the carpets with as much green waste as we could collect. When all this had rotted down a bit, we would plant the legume tagasaste, a short-lived nitrogen-fixing shrub, together with mānuka which would be the 'pioneer crop' that would provide shelter for the main crop of native plants. The budget for all this was estimated at $37,808 — no problem at all.

We created a booklet to send to potential sponsors and printed it on recycled matt paper — this was not an occasion to be glossy. The cover was a soft brown with the title, 'an inner-city forest', all lower case, enclosed in a small black square. There was a dramatic aerial photo on the first page that accentuated the motorway system in its snake-like glory, and showed the school as a brave outpost perched precariously above it. The benefits for children, community and the world were extolled, letters of support attached and, somewhere, apologetic mention of the need for $37,808.

We sent the booklet to a number of companies and charities that we thought might be environmentally inclined and cash-loaded. I held my breath and attempted to keep the nagging voices of reality at bay. Within a month, our appeal was oversubscribed. Oversubscribed! I could draw breath again. It became the only educational project I was ever involved in that had enough money. Probably not enough in the end, but that was because we became more ambitious. I don't really know why people gave so freely. This was 1993, and conservation and the threat of global warming were not at the front of people's minds. The film *An Inconvenient Truth* was not released until 2006, but maybe people had some inkling of what it was going to show. Perhaps the idea of children, native trees and a community joining together to make a forest held some intrinsic appeal. Perhaps? But reasons don't matter. The thing is it worked, and we had support.

As soon as we were ready, we asked kaumātua from Ngāti Whātua o Ōrākei and Tainui to hold a whakatuwhera, a dawn blessing. Listening to karakia and shuffling through the early-morning light with a large proportion of the school community somehow magnified the hope that successful fundraising had started.

The first stage involved asking carpet layers to drop off their old used carpets. They did this with enthusiasm, and we soon had a minor carpet mountain. I had contacted the Corrections Department and they'd agreed that laying out the carpets was an okay project for people sentenced to community service to undertake. They were an invaluable source of labour. I talked to the first group and attempted to outline the scope and purpose of the project. Their nods of agreement and sparks of enthusiasm were soon extinguished when they discovered the carpets were heavy and still had a few random tacks lying in wait for their hands. Gloves helped this problem, but there was no getting away from the difficulty of weight and steepness. Some of the supervisors thought the job might have been too tough; others thought it was not tough enough.

Once the carpets were in place, we contacted several landscape contractors and asked them to drop their green waste at our lower carpark. Their enthusiasm was astonishing, as was the way the word spread that this was a free foliage dump. The mountain of branches and prunings outgrew the carpark and spilled onto the road. There were complaints from local businesses about the risk of fire and rats, and how the haystacks we had made would attract local prostitutes. Some mentioned our children — their noise, their behaviour, their colour and their immigration status. I gave the complainants our fundraising booklet and suggested they might feel better about the project if they participated in it. Again, I employed the mathematics-teacher look and words the English teacher would have frowned upon.

Rather than wait for the next round of community service labour, we hired a man with a bobcat, and the foliage covered the slope in a short space of time. The next stage was not so shortlived. There was a long wait for the material to rot down enough to allow for planting, and it was about six months before we were able to plant out thousands of tagasaste and mānuka.

The bank looked scruffy and untidy for the next few years as the straggly tagasaste took hold. Neighbours, folk living on the other side of motorway with a view of our grounds, and people from the ERO tended to say things like 'About time you did something about that unsightly bank, don't you think, Tim? Get rid of the rubbish and mow it perhaps?' These people received the last copies of the fundraising booklet.

In May 1995 we were able to start the proper planting. Young trees had been gathered from the nurseries of Auckland City Council, Project Crimson and sundry other sources big and small. We had also set up a nursery at the school, and the permaculture students showed the children how to plant seeds and nurture young plants.

We held a series of planting working bees on several Saturday mornings. My theory about working bees is that you start early, you try to get tons of people, and you make sure you are able to give them each a task and the gear to do it — there's nothing worse than having volunteers hanging around when they could have been home doing some pressing task. At midday you give them a hot sausage and a cold beer and send them home, ideally full of happy stories and a desire to do more. A civic-minded cricket mate used to say, 'You have to go to all the working bees and all the funerals!' We spread the word far and wide, and at the first working bee at least a hundred people turned up. For a while, the school became a joyous village, hard work alleviated by laughter and a sense of togetherness. Happily, my plan to send them home at midday didn't fully work and people stayed till mid-afternoon, chatting and finishing extra tasks they had set themselves. I went around grinning for weeks.

By the time enthusiasm started to wane, most of the planting had been done. We had a nervous summer, hoping everything would survive. Most of it did — and those who had prayed for rain felt vindicated. I was not among their number but was happy to give them credit, just in case. The forest flourished. I think everybody felt a sense of joy to see young pōhutukawa, kauri and pūriri poke their heads above the artificial forest floor we had created. Gradually, the tagasaste died out, their job done, the trees loving the nitrogen they left behind.

It was not, of course, a total success. Children did not respond as positively as I hoped to time spent in the plant nursery area. The wait for seeds to germinate was a bit too long to sustain their interest. They had, however, all planted a tree or two. It is my hope that this experience meant they grew up knowing that planting trees was something they could and wanted to do. Some critics of the project remained: people who told me all we had done was to make a haven for muggers and rapists, pessimists who thought locals would cut down the trees for firewood, and parents who wondered out loud if projects like this were what a school should be doing. Others mentioned fire and children getting lost. But these were a minority, and they did not stop the forest from flourishing.

Today, when I have a 'what's it all about, Alfie?' moment, I go and walk along the paths Leon made, gaze up at the trees that now tower above me and, somehow, I feel so much better.

20.

THERE WERE VERY FEW Māori children at Kaikohe Primary School when I was there in 1947 — they were supposed to go to the 'Native School' up the hill. There was among the rest of us the feeling that Māori shouldn't be at 'our' school at all. Sometimes they spoke to each other in te reo Māori. We knew this was a bad thing, so we told on them and they were punished. I grew up believing that things Māori were bad, especially the language. I remember being told that a couple were 'getting married' and mishearing it as 'getting Maoried', and I felt devastated for them.

These feelings, this upbringing, changed, but slowly and without much encouragement to make changes. My father, a kind and humble man, was benevolently patronising towards other races. He was capable of saying, 'Unlike the rest of them she is a wonderful housewife — you could eat your dinner off her floor.' He was also capable of saying, when I left a task undone for him to do, 'When did your last nigger die?'

Teachers may not have used the same language, but they

did not promote anything Māori, apart from some songs and stick games. My eyes started to open, as I believe they did for many, when I began reading the wonderful *School Journals*. In one of them I found a version of the Parihaka story, and was both horrified and fascinated – who were the bad guys? At secondary school we were taught the history of the 'Māori Wars' and some of us began to ask questions.

By the time I reached university I had read enough to know that injustices had been done, changes had to be made, and the least I could do would be to learn some of the language. I took Māori Studies and was taught by Bruce Biggs, Pat Hohepa, Robert Mahuta and Pita Sharples. Did I realise how lucky I was? Probably not, but what I did relish was that this was the first time I could talk with others about Māori issues, rather than just read about them. I had befriended a Ngāti Porou couple who lived down the road, Mary and Darnie Walker, and would visit them often for lessons in pronunciation and beer drinking. By the time I reached teachers' college I knew I wanted to promote te reo Māori as much as I could. Having said that, my classroom ambitions were modest: too much for those above me, but not nearly enough to make any real difference. In most of my classrooms I put charts on the walls of numbers, the Māori alphabet and days of the week. We would spend a little bit of time trying to perfect pronunciation of place names, and that was about it.

When I started at Newton Central I knew I wanted to make Māori language a priority, but I also knew that if we were to go beyond the small efforts I had already made, I would have to wait for a request to come from the community. In the first few years, there was no such request. More than that, there was a widespread 'I did not bring my children to New Zealand to learn Māori' sentiment. This was strongly expressed at a board of trustees meeting by a gentleman from the Pacific who was also a Mormon bishop. He railed against the increasing number of Māori elements creeping into classrooms and school protocols. He also made an impassioned speech about all the payments he saw on financial reports going to 'School Pubs'. It was some time before we could interrupt his anti-booze tirade and apologise for not writing 'Publications' in full.

I made public my desire to establish a Māori bilingual unit as soon as parents requested it, but it was several years before such a request arrived. Then my delight was tempered by the pragmatic question of how we would start. The start came when I was able to persuade Charlie, a parent who spoke Māori whenever he could, to come to take lessons with groups who wanted them. Charlie was cheerful, humble and locked into the teaching style that had been inflicted on him when he was at school. We worked on this, but without completely winning his heart and soul. He was at school when the Review Office visited. One of their number came to me with shock and horror all over his face. 'The Māori guy with all the tats. I think he might have been in a gang!' Clearly, I was supposed to instantly dismiss Charlie, but asked about his teaching instead. The answer suggested that the question may have not been relevant.

Within a year there was sufficient interest to form a bilingual unit. What's more, we had a teacher employed to run the class. She was a lovely, kind person with a strong te reo background.

Unfortunately, she found classroom organisation a bit too much of a challenge. This was the beginning of a realisation that should have been obvious: what we needed was someone with both pedagogical skills and depth in te reo. We gave whatever support we could, and kept hoping for the miracle of the rare person with both of these attributes to come along.

And she did.

Hoana Pearson was teaching at neighbouring Grey Lynn Primary. She rang me one day and asked to come over for a kōrero during her lunchtime. This meeting had, in some ways, all the characteristics of a successful first date, in that we instantly fell into areas of common interest and enthusiasm. The lunchtime flew by, words tumbling and sparkling, optimism filling the room. I had found the teacher I was looking for; she had found the school she was looking for. Within a term, she left Grey Lynn and came to work with us. Initially, this was in tandem with the other teacher, then, quite soon, on her own.

Those who have worked in schools — worked anywhere, perhaps — will not be deceived by the apparent simplicity of the previous sentence. Helping a struggling teacher change is a task that involves time, understanding and emotional stamina. Sadly, it is seldom successful. There is, I think, an element in all good teachers that cannot be taught. The intuitive understanding of how to interact with children, the feelings of joy teaching can bring, and the capacity for hard work, are either there or not. Training can be given, should be given, but in the absence of these intuitions to some degree at least, training has to become too detailed, too painting-by-numbers, too prescribed — all of which is a long-winded way of saying good teachers have a special innate talent. It is also hard not to think that the detailed, prescriptive syllabus of today, together with the demand to have written evaluation of almost every move, will override and rein in anything innate.

Hoana had, still has, an extraordinary talent for teaching and a passionate dedication to te reo. Her working-class background and her struggle to overcome the economic and racist barriers to her obtaining a higher education had made her a champion of the underdog and a fighter for justice. She ran the bilingual unit with respect for kaupapa Māori and the principles of good teaching. It was more than a joy to behold; it was a model for others to learn from.

The unit was a place where parents came and went freely, where they participated in monthly hui, and had an involvement in decision-making that would possibly be beneficial in all classrooms. I say 'possibly' because these parents had a strong uniting bond in their desire for their children to learn Māori. In other settings there would probably be too many divergent views and agendas for such a meeting to be as positive and harmonious as these ones generally were.

Good teaching demands a huge amount of work. In a bilingual setting, in the 1990s, the demand was even higher. There was a paucity of resources, and Hoana and her pupils' families spent hours making them. She had a habit of using a ruler to guide her marker pen when she was creating posters and books. This gave them a characteristic straightness, but she would need to go back and add the tails to letters that needed them. It amused me that someone so dedicated to the dotting of i's and the crossing of t's would sometimes leave g, j, p, q and y oddly truncated.

The lot of people teaching in bilingual classes was often an unsupported one. They were usually assigned a room at the back of the school, given a bunch of kids of all ages and told to get on with it. A box in the ERO list of requirements had been ticked and the school could focus on other matters. I like to think we provided a high level of support, not least because all our classes were family-grouped. The 'Māori class' wasn't an isolated ambassador for multi-level teaching. In addition, the other teachers had sufficient idealism to accept having a few extra children in their classrooms so that the numbers in the bilingual unit could be kept low.

We were proud of this unit. I loved being there, hearing the words and observing how well organised everything was, but I knew we hadn't gone far enough. Everything I had read and experienced told me we had to create a full-immersion unit, a term, like so many in education, that I couldn't quite let sit comfortably. Whenever it is used, images of the River Jordan pop into my head.

I had made several attempts in my life to come to terms with other languages. At school I went to classes in French, Latin and German. All I remember from these is confusion and one German phrase: *Warum fürhen Sie den Hund nicht an der Leine?* ('Why don't you keep your dog on a lead?') To my disappointment, I have never found occasion to use it.

Māori Studies at university was better, in that my motivation was higher and the tutors encouraged speaking rather than reading. However, my most successful language-learning experience was in Sāmoa. Siainiu spoke immaculate English, but most people in the village knew little beyond the odd significant phrase like 'All Blacks'. In three months, immersion and necessity taught me enough to get by. We tend to learn vocabulary around special interests, and, as I've revealed before, I acquired lots of words to do with child raising. I also discovered that the step from adequacy to accuracy is a big one that I never really took. It was enough to say, 'Go bus this Apia?' to receive the answer I was looking for, and I was too lazy to do better. However, I did learn that being surrounded by the language was an exponentially better way for me to learn. This was what we had to do if we wanted real progress in Māori language learning, especially in a world where children were bombarded with English.

Again, the trigger was a request from parents. Another couple, both working in academic jobs, a bit radical and totally dedicated to te reo, made an appointment to see me to discuss what would happen to one of their children who was about to leave kōhanga reo and come to our school. They, too, believed that immersion was the only way to go. Here I feel compelled to say that I was approached many times, over my years as a principal, by people wanting change. Many of these requests began with 'A friend who came around for coffee said you should...' or 'I heard on talkback radio you should...' One parent had actually stood at the school gate with a petition calling for me to be removed from the school. She got a bit cross when I asked if I could sign it too.

The three times parents made requests for us to do more in terms of Māori language I was impressed by how well researched and presented the cases they made were. They asked with humility and courtesy, with the patience of those who had been compelled to wait. I agreed with the couple who wanted a total-immersion unit to be created, but knew there were many practical difficulties. Would Hoana be willing to take on this role? Would she be able to become deputy principal, as I wanted her to, if she had the demands of such a class to run? How would the board of trustees and the other teachers receive the suggestion? Did we have an appropriate space? Would there be enough parents wanting this type of learning for their children? Initially, all these questions seemed too hard, but everything fell into place easily, as if it was meant to be, and the immersion unit 'Te Uru Karaka' was born.

This unit became a focal point of the school and we looked towards it for leadership in the te reo programmes in the other classrooms and in the school ceremonies. A Pākehā neighbour who had enrolled his five-year-old daughter in the school reported to me that she asked, one night after she had been with us for about six months, 'Why aren't we as important as the Māori children?' Of course I wanted all children to feel important, but it did please me that there was a perception that Māori kids, so long at the bottom of the heap, had gained mana in the school setting. I probably spent too much time just standing, watching, absorbed in Te Uru Karaka, happy to see it in action, regretful that my little school at Papuni hadn't been like this, that all the Māori kids I had taught hadn't had this opportunity to have their language reawakened in them, hadn't felt valued because they were Māori.

21.

I CANNOT LEAVE words about Newton Central School without adding more about three memorable and significant people. The first is Dianne. I can't say she was the best teacher I ever met, because teachers are 'best' in so many different ways. Nonetheless, she was the best. Dianne worked huge hours and prepared in the kind of detail that is possible only if a teacher has deep knowledge of her pupils. She intuitively knew what they each wanted and was hard on herself if she felt she was not providing it. Despite the workload, she was always kind and patient. Over and above everything else, she had a natural, spontaneous sense of humour that permeated her whole day. Her class had fun; the kids would laugh with the freedom of those who know they are loved, safe and valued. She was such a good teacher that I wanted to see her promoted. I talked with her about what she wanted to do next. She told me she wanted to leave teaching and get a job in a supermarket stacking shelves, to rediscover her mind and go home at five o'clock every day. She never did.

I needed a new secretary, two wonderful secretaries having resigned because they found bigger and better things to do. I wanted someone who would be warm and welcoming to visitors, knowledgeable about the community and able to pronounce Pasifika names correctly. I asked one of the parents, Maryann Poi, to consider the job. She declined. She could not type, she had no educational qualifications, she had never done an important job, and she was certain to disappoint me and the school. I told her we wanted her for the person she was, and that we would train her to type and to acquire whatever other skills became necessary. With trepidation she accepted, and I am sure her first few months in the job were stressful, even overwhelming. Her usual quiet smile was replaced by frowns and worry lines. As I write, almost thirty-five years later, she is still there, in control, confident, a smiling and highly competent source of reassurance to successive principals.

Daryl came to see me one Monday morning. He was a big lad, long black hair oiled into a ponytail, large safety pins in his ears, asymmetrical tattoos with sharp corners, and a tee shirt that read: 'Life's a Shit Then You Die'. He talked in a clear, articulate way. He had been sentenced to community service hours for unpaid fines, and wondered if he could work them off at the school. I liked him straight away and agreed. And then had misgivings – a little intuition is a wonderful and dangerous thing.

He did a series of maintenance and gardening jobs with competence, skill and initiative. We talked a lot, and he revealed a range of ideas and knowledge that caused me to call him a 'closet intellectual'. He had a band called Malevolence.

He told me that if I needed to give it a classification I could call it 'Gothic Punk'. Our caretaker left, and I offered Daryl the job. For the next fifteen years he was caretaker and then property manager, dealing with officials and issues with calm confidence and common sense. I wish I had been able to tell David Lange.

I met Daryl at a poetry gig a few years ago. He was wearing a suit and told me about the job he had at a technical institute, lecturing in acoustic engineering. He introduced me to his friends as the person who had saved his life, which caused me to gaze into my beer for a very long time.

IF THE FOREST, the way the school was humming along and the joy of seeing meaningful te reo learning were all sources of contentment, the same could not be said of my home life. Peter had returned from two years with his uncle in Sāmoa, a little scarred emotionally and physically from the experience. He had once been on a bus travelling through a village where warring factions were throwing stones at each other. A stone came through where the window would have been if there was a window, and hit him above the eye, opening a large gash. His aunt gave him a slap for being at the wrong place at the wrong time. His language and cultural immersion experience had not been easy, but it helped on the journey of coming to terms with his background and, perhaps, the death of the mother who would have cemented and nurtured both sides of that background. Lope, a successful academic, was embarking on legal studies and a demanding law career. Neither of them really felt comfortable with the partner I had chosen to marry. She was a fundamentally good person, but two young adult part-Sāmoan stepchildren and a husband with odd educational ideals were not how she wanted life to be. Step-parenting has its difficulties and, as James Thurber once said, stepmothers are a sadly misunderstood class of people. This may be true, but I know it doesn't work unless you are able to make a 100 per cent commitment to it. The unspoken, immutable unity and understanding between the children and me must have seemed like an impenetrable exclusion zone to her. I spoke of accepting her being a supportive flatmate but, in truth, I don't think this would have eased my restless discontent.

The marriage broke up with more acrimony than I thought possible. I was overwhelmed with a sense of loss, shame and failure. One day at school Greg gently asked me about how I was feeling. I broke down, overwhelmed by what was happening and the memory of all the times I had faced the end of relationships, the breaking of things I should have nurtured or never touched. He persuaded me to take the day off.

I didn't want to go home, so I went to the pictures in a theatre with that empty feeling that theatres have at eleven in the morning. The movie was *Once Were Warriors* – sometimes we make very bad choices. I had been advised to see this movie by one of the parents, Darren. He was a big ex-gang member who brought his children to school every day, his face one big gentle smile. His speech patterns suggested he had been hit on the head more than once.

'Ya gotta see that fulm *Once Were Warriors*, Tum. Gotta see it! Gotta, Tum.'

'Why?' I asked. 'What makes it so good?'

'Reality, man. It's reality. That's why. Reality.'

I had, some months before, gone to school one Monday morning with a black eye. A cricket ball I was fielding had hit an unexpected bump, bounced up and slapped me. When Darren saw me, he put his large hand on my shoulder.

'Back-up, Tum, any time you need back-up jus' say the word. Jus' say the word.'

Unlike everyone else who had seen my black eye, he wasn't joking.

My wife left, taking many of our possessions with her, including the CD of Kiri Te Kanawa singing Puccini arias that, together with red wine, I had used to fuel my 'poor me' feelings. Peter and I lived in the house, flatmates and mates. He and Lope would take me out. They tried to find places we would all enjoy. The best was a local pool hall. It, along with their obvious caring, did the trick, and I bounced back to tattered optimism more rapidly than was probably decent.

Around this time Deborah, who had a six-year-old at the school, invited me to a barbecue at her place. We lived in the same street, and I assumed the barbecue was a kind of meet-the-neighbours gathering. She was a medical doctor working at a local GP clinic. I had always thought she was cool, always enjoyed talking with her, and had, perhaps, engineered times to talk with her more often than school matters demanded. I enjoyed the barbecue and the company of her friends, and thought a guy who teamed up with this kind and clever woman would be a very lucky guy.

Somehow, in the following week, we went to the movies

together and saw, prophetically or otherwise, *Heavenly Creatures*. A few days later, Deborah drove to Wellington to spend some time with her widowed father who lived in a huge, splendid, comfortably ageing house by the sea at Karaka Bay. I wrote her a long letter — something we did before email eroded romance. I addressed it to 'Debra', a version of her name used by several children at school. John, her dad, a lovely erudite man who would become a dear friend, took it to her with the words, 'You have a letter from someone who can't spell.' He was more than disconcerted when he discovered I was his grandson's school principal.

To cut a short story even shorter, I flew to Wellington so Deborah and I could share each other's company on the drive back to Auckland. Six weeks later we purchased a house together. Lope the lawyer was horrified and came around to counsel caution. It is a brave and significant step in the parent–child relationship when the child gives specific adult advice, rather than the wide-ranging suggestions for improvement of the teenage years. We did not heed it, but loved her even more for giving it.

The father of Deborah's son Rupert was Sāmoan. Rupert, Lope and Peter all look more like each other than any of them look like either of us, much to their delight. Deborah and I have now been together for twenty-six years, twenty-four of them in a marriage that has, I believe, encouraged both of us to grow — she is now a successful and highly valued child and adolescent psychiatrist, and I have reinvented myself as a word dabbler and mildly successful poet. I will leave you to guess which of us funds the operation.

ABOUT THE TIME Deborah and I threw our lives together, my dream of an urban school made up of family-grouped classrooms and child-centred programmes started to fall apart. Staff changes meant that we had some people uncomfortable and unsuccessful with family grouping. I couldn't be bothered with aspects of the paperwork and was duly rubbished by the ERO. I had neither the time nor the inclination to assemble a proper counter to their demands.

In many schools the deputy principal is released from the classroom to do both the one hundred and one small things that happen each day and to work on writing down the obvious so others can see we know about it. Hoana was appointed to this position when Greg left to spread the New Zealand educational gospel in the United States. Hoana was working full-time, and then some, in the immersion unit, as well as keeping an eye on the bilingual unit. This was real teaching, and I was not going to take her away from it. I had what I wanted, but I did not have the services of an experienced non-teaching deputy. We make our choices and need to accept the consequences. In this case, it was a paucity of paperwork – I would make the same decision again.

Quite suddenly, at the end of 1998, I realised that I had had enough, that I was becoming grumpy and disillusioned, that the capacity in me that allowed me to teach was at its end. I had recurrent thoughts of the tired old teachers we had vowed never to become when we were starry-eyed teachers' college students. In addition, Deb and I were both too busy. The demands on her as a GP were endless. There were many Friday evenings when she would come home late and exhausted, I would be equally spent, and we would just sit and look at each other. It had been fun, her being the local doctor, me being the local school principal, but it had meant that even going to the local supermarket was a long-drawn-out process where selecting tins of baked beans was interspersed with a series of mini consultations about reading and some quite intimate medical matters people were so eager to discuss that the public nature of the discussion did not seem to matter.

Lope and Peter were producing the first of our nine grandchildren, and Rupert was just starting at Kōwhai Intermediate School. It felt like our family needed more of our time — not just time, but time that could be freely and cheerfully given. In addition, we were about to start the renovations to our very tired old villa. When we had rushed into buying it six years earlier we had said to each other it was just liveable but that we would have to do it up before the end of the year.

One of us needed to stay home, and I put my hand up very quickly, claiming that I was a better cook, that I could help the builder, that doctors earned more than teachers and that I was older anyway. So, I resigned. It was just like that — a short sentence, no calamity or angst, just the feeling that I was doing the right thing, that my teaching career had come to an end.

Or so I believed.

I loved working on the house with Gus the builder, a laconic and skilful man with extraordinary physical strength. He was patient with my shortcomings, and I think we worked out a good and companionable working relationship. One of the many things I learned in the six months it took to get the house right was that just as managerial demands had stopped me playing in the mud with children, so too did the paperwork of a building project stop me from picking up my hammer and making satisfying noises. Building inspectors and council rule-makers quickly replaced the ERO as figures I wanted to stick pins into.

There were wonderful days, however, when we had all the supplies we needed, and I would cut timber and Gus would fix it in place. If there were any cuts that were a bit wobbly or mildly inaccurate, he would write 'Tim did this' on them before nailing them in place. I desperately wanted to be able to write 'Gus did this', but there was never an opportunity. Physical work, the Steve's gate tangibility of the work, was the best therapy possible, and did much to help me recognise and deal with the grief I felt at leaving Newton Central.

I also had a contract with the Ministry of Education to work with a Decile One school that was deemed to be failing. This was enjoyable, stimulating work, all the more so because Rose, the school's principal, was a teacher and administrator of intelligence, passion and skill. She was turning the school around, but was hamstrung by debt incurred by a previous board of trustees and by promises of help from the Ministry that never materialised. My regular mandatory reports to the Ministry stated that the school's main problem was the Ministry. My contract was not renewed.

I worked with the board for a while longer on a voluntary basis, trying to finalise some of the projects we had started. One of the school's main problems was security. Almost every night it was broken into. The copper guttering was stolen.

Nothing of value could be left out in classrooms. The grounds needed to be securely fenced, as I advised the Ministry repeatedly. The official I reported to arranged for a security guard to be posted each night. I chatted one evening with one of these guards, a young woman who brought her baby to work. She said they were there all night but stayed locked in her car, as far away from the marauding youths as she could be. The Ministry said we were free to spend the money we had set aside to build a modern library/information centre to build a fence if we so desired. This was the freedom of choice Tomorrow's Schools had granted us. We argued that the special safety issues of the school should not mean we had to go without a library.

The situation became impossible when Rose reluctantly resigned and went to another school where she could focus on teaching. The board resigned. The school was closed and the Ministry took control of the place. The first thing they did was to build a fence. Not just a fence, but a magnificent fence with specifications well above what I had visualised. I go and gaze at that fence every now and then, just to remind myself that there will always be windmills to tilt at.

JUST AS MY STINT as a builder's labourer/project manager was coming to an end, I received a phone call from a friend in the Correspondence School. There was a gap in the home-visiting team in Auckland. He had heard I was just hanging about banging in nails and banging away at the Ministry of Education. Maybe I would like to return to this work for a month or two while a permanent appointment was made? My delight in accepting might have been tempered had I known the job would go on for the next four years.

The contract required spending a week each term in Wellington, meeting teachers and being instructed about what was currently important. I would stay with other guys doing the same job: Phil, my Auckland colleague, Russell from Dunedin and Ewan from Christchurch. Dave, a science teacher at the school, usually joined us. He was a robust rebel of unquenchable humour, tragically killed in a tramping accident a few years later.

Suffice it to say, these times produced more laughter than the rest of my teaching years put together. I think we did useful work, but for me there was a difference between putting up my hand for a job and yelling 'I'm the best person, so pick me' and being asked to fill a supposedly temporary gap. I tried not to make waves, and I made sure I gave home more time, except when I was seeing students on Great Barrier or at the far end of the Coromandel Peninsula.

During this and another two-year stint with the school several years later, I became disillusioned about the token nature of so much of the work. The idea of working with a small number of kids and helping them towards a positive future was talked about, but not enough practical steps were taken. I used my image of the obligation to keep watering seeds planted in a desert so many times that people would go, 'Yes, yes, yes, we know ...' as soon as I started. In contrast with the School Certificate days of my earlier employment, I loved the fact that NCEA could give kids some concrete achievements.

Nobody got sixty-four Excellences before Christmas, as I heard successful day-school students claim, but at least they got something to show for their efforts.

I visited Paremoremo prison a number of times, wanting to support the enthusiastic and skilful education officer (i.e. teacher) who worked there. I looked through one prisoner's work with him and became excited about the quality of what he was doing. The following conversation ensued.

Me: This is great work, mate.

Him: Thank you, Sir. I like the work. Like doing it.

Me: You are doing so well I want to bump you up a few levels.

Him: Why would you do that, Sir?

Me: Well, at the level I am thinking about, you could start to collect NCEA credits. And call me Tim, not Sir.

Him: Why would I want them, Sir?

Me: Well, um, well one day you will leave this place and the credits will be something you have in your hand, something that will show others what you are capable of doing.

Him: Why would I want to do that?

Me: Well, it would be so good to have when you apply for a job, something to show the boss, something to —

Him: A job? If I had a job I'd have a boss, and if I had a boss one day he'd say something that pissed me off and when he did that I'd stick a bloody knife into him. So, what say I just study for the joy of learning, don't you think, Sir?

Me: (speechless)

I started to understand that NCEA was not to everyone's taste.

I became acting manager of the twelve teachers who visited

students in the regions. I enjoyed the work but ran into conflict with TCS management, mainly about how restructuring, version three, affected the people in my team. The needs of urban kids were not, to my mind and observation, being addressed realistically. There had been moves to give greater support to those who needed it, but these didn't go far enough to make any real difference. I became embroiled in a difficult and bitter conflict with the CEO. She thought I was sabotaging her; I thought she was ambushing me. Probably, we were both right.

I left in a huff. My contract was given to someone with zero experience and that was it.

My teaching career was over, almost as accidentally as it had started.

Epilogue

I BELIEVE I HAVE been a positive influence in the lives of many children, and this gives me satisfaction, albeit a satisfaction to be balanced against knowing that there were many children for whom I was not the right person. I feel sad and guilty about those who were in my care during the years in which I struggled to survive and did not have enough left in me to be a proper teacher.

I want more people to become teachers.

We are, all of us, already teachers in one way and measure or another. This is true especially of parents, but also of everything we do with workmates, with kids in sports teams, with the driver who turned right when he had indicated left, with people who voted for the other party and who think they can be convincing when they have only half the facts.

I want more people to go to teachers' colleges and work towards having groups of children to be with, and to learn with and from. I want this because teaching, despite the conflicts and disappointments catalogued in this book, has for me been a source of joy — well, intermittent joy. The joy is being with someone when their brain lines up all the ducks necessary to be able to read, or to become comfortable with numbers, or to run around the block faster than ever before.

I have spoken with several young teachers currently beavering away at what we used to call 'the chalk face', a term like so many that has become redundant in my lifetime. They spoke of a disconnect with management. They seemed to accept a regime of test, evaluate and report that would have driven me to despair. They know they are not allowed to take children outside every hour, or catch the equivalent of the Farmers free bus, or go anywhere, for that matter, without filling in many forms and enlisting an army of helpers. We spoke about salaries. They expressed deep frustration that the job they spend sixty to seventy hours a week trying to satisfy does not enable them to buy a house, as I had, for twice their annual salary.

Despite all this, they talked of their love of being with children. They might not yet have understood that through their work they were supposed to solve the shortcomings of parents and the ills of society. Their joy at seeing children learn burned brightly and will continue to do so for that finite period of time in which they will be the best of teachers.

I want our society to honour and trust them, to pay them enough to house themselves, to recognise what they know and what is in their hearts without insistence on regimes that stifle their creativity and reduce children to measurable units. I want art in the morning, maths in the afternoon and music all day long. I want children to run with the same exuberance with which my dog runs, just for the delight of it. And then I want them to run a bit further and faster the next day. I want all children and teachers to look at other children and to be able to say, despite what failings and difficulties they have, 'She or he is just a regular kid.' I want them to be able to yell and shout at each other in at least the two languages of Aotearoa. I want them to walk to school.

I want chronological age to be ignored, learning to read to be a leisurely process, and the legacy of the missionaries left to rest in peace.

I want kids to again be allowed to play bullrush.

Author's Note

I HAVE, FOR the most part, used real names of children and adults. In these cases, my words and feelings about them are (and were) positive. I trust that if these people read the book, seeing their names will cause them to smile.

Some names, however, have been changed. This is because what I have written could be construed as critical, or the person is, in fact, based on several people. There are other cases when, much to my shame, I have had to use a made-up name because I have forgotten the real one.

Acknowledgements

IT HAS BEEN often said – perhaps too often – that it takes a village to raise a child. If this is true, and I believe it is, then it is also true that it takes a small town to support the author of a book. I intend to name and thank fellow citizens of this town, all of whom, in one way or another, made the creation of this book possible.

This list starts, as it always must, with family. I thank Deb, who is always encouraging, albeit at times with comments like 'Why are you attempting to repair that mower/fence/leaking tap/hole in the wall? You write so well, but fixing things? Perhaps not . . .' Despite being a psychiatrist, she clearly doesn't fully understand procrastination. It is also true that the fact Deb has a proper job means I have time to write and to attempt to fix things. Our children, if that term can be used for successful grown-up people, have given practical advice and shown unwarranted faith in my abilities. I thank Peter, Mardi, Lope, Sharon, Rupert and Sophie. Sophie was a promising critical reader until my baby granddaughter

Rory made it clear that reading was a luxury not permitted to young mothers.

I have been a member of a writing group that grew, some twenty years ago, out of classes run by the late David Lyndon Brown. David's example and his gentle teaching gave me belief that my enthusiasm for writing, expressed up until that point only through school newsletters, was not a waste of time. This group – Sally Monks, Barbara Austin, Tony O'Brien and Christine Tyler – have provided invaluable critical comment along the way. The insightfulness of these comments and the encouragement embodied in the group have been hugely helpful.

My second writing group, known as 'Klatch', grew out of the Masters in Creative Writing course conducted by John Cranna in 2008. At this course I met Rod Fee, Judith White, Katie Henderson, Ann Glamuzina and Karen Breen. These people have become not just writing buddies, but also close friends. We try to meet once a week for coffee, writing, criticism of writing and gossip. If I have grown as a writer, thanks have to go to this group. Under Rod's leadership, they formed the successful and innovative Eunoia Publishing Group, which published my poetry collection *Not as the Crow Flies* in 2018. This collection was edited by Judith White, from whom I continue to learn so much. I thank Josephine Stanton and Juliet Batten for invaluable reading and comments.

Poetry, in many ways my first love, has contributed much to whatever skills I have as a writer. I am indebted to Poetry Live, the weekly pub-based poetry evening that has lurched along on its riotous way for the past forty years. It is a collection of like (and unlike) minds, always willing to lend an interested ear to new poets and to delight, usually, with their own work.

Audience response is a forge that encourages and disciplines. I want to thank two heroes of the Auckland performance poetry scene: Penny Ashton and Ken Arkind. Penny, herself a superb performer, was the organiser and irreverent MC of the famous Poetry Idol Slam that was, for many years, such a feature of the Auckland Writers Festival. This evening of competitive poetry was a fearful but uplifting challenge for people like me, who are (or were) more accustomed to poetry as a fireside activity. Ken continues to be an ambassador for poetry, encouraging so many young folk to write and giving older ones a stage to stumble on. And I cannot mention poetry without mentioning my dear friend and poet Penny Somerville, who has read so much of my work, nodding sagely – sometimes in approval.

Jenny Hellen, publishing director at Allen & Unwin, asked me to write this book and organised proper writerly things like contracts, deadlines and advances. I think only writers will fully appreciate the implications of that sentence and the words 'asked me'. Writers are wallflowers, seldom asked, and so grateful when they are. Jenny's encouragement along the way has been invaluable, as was the selection of Jane Parkin to edit the book. Stephen King allegedly once said 'All editors are divine!' This may or may not be true, and it does hint at their power, but it is unarguably true that Jane, with her skill, perception and ability to correct without diminishing, is a literary angel. Senior editor Leanne McGregor has applied the same excellence to the book, in the relentless pursuit of accuracy and completeness.

I thank the rest of the Allen & Unwin team, especially publicity manager Abba Renshaw, marketing manager Courtney Smith, and Melanie Laville-Moore and Nyssa Walsh in the sales department. I also thank freelance designer Saskia Nicol, the aforementioned and worshipped Jane Parkin, and freelance proofreaders Kate Stone and Teresa McIntyre. Having a team like this behind me has made writing both more rigorous and more satisfying than ever before.

Harry Ricketts, Hoana Pearson, Judith White, Sharon Hawke and Tony O'Brien — all successful, busy, talented people — read the first proof and made comments. Their generosity with time, the kindness of their comments and their willingness to let their remarks be used for publicity are deeply appreciated.

Special thanks to Ma'ilo Usuga I'iga and Rosalina Siō, who reviewed my use of Sāmoan words, changing the written approximations of someone who had learned by listening into an acceptable written form.

I cannot fail to acknowledge photographer Jane Ussher, who triumphed over the limitations of the raw material when shooting my author photo, and who is such a lovely person to spend a chatty morning with.

Finally, I thank my dog Stella, who has spent many hours at my feet listening to me tap the keyboard and greeting the passages I have read to her with silent approval.

Bibliography

Ashton-Warner, Sylvia, *Teacher*, New York: Simon and Schuster, 1963.

Baldwin, James, *Another Country*, New York: Dial Press, 1962.

Beeby, Clarence, *The Biography of an Idea: Beeby on Education*, Wellington: New Zealand Council for Educational Research, 1992.

Bloomfield, Leonard, *Language*, New York: Henry Holt, 1933.

Buller, Walter Lawry, *A History of the Birds of New Zealand*, illustrated by J G Keulemans, 2nd edn, vol. 1, Schleswig-Holstein: Hansebooks, 2017 (an unchanged, high-quality reprint of the original two-volume edition of 1888).

Chomsky, Noam, *Aspects of the Theory of Syntax*, Cambridge, MA: MIT Press, 1965.

Golding, William, *The Lord of the Flies*, London: Faber & Faber, 1954.

Holm, Anne, *I Am David*, translated from the Danish by L W Kingsland, London: Methuen Children's Books, 1965.

Hunn, J K, *Report on Department of Maori Affairs*, Wellington: Government Printer, 1961.

O'Dell, Scott, *Island of the Blue Dolphins*, Boston, MA: Houghton Mifflin, 1960.

Paton, Alan, *Cry, the Beloved Country*, London: Jonathan Cape, 1948.

Raine, Kathleen, *The Collected Poems of Kathleen Raine*, London: Hamish Hamilton, 1956.

Read, Herbert, *Education Through Art*, London: Faber & Faber, 1943.

Richardson, Elwyn S, *In the Early World*, Wellington: New Zealand Council for Educational Research, 1964.

Seredy, Kate, *The Good Master*, New York: The Viking Press, 1935.

Williams, William, *A Dictionary of the New Zealand Language, and a Concise Grammar; to which is added a selection of colloquial sentences*, London: Williams and Norgate, 1852.

About the Author

Author photograph by Jane Ussher

TIM HEATH STUMBLED into teachers' college in 1962 and became hooked by the joy and challenge of teaching. He taught for the next forty-seven years in a variety of roles and places, including remote rural New Zealand and a village on Sāmoa's second island, Savai'i. Some of his teaching was in secondary schools, but he mainly worked in primary schools, where he became fascinated with children's initial experience of school and how they learn to read. For a time, he became an educational gypsy, visiting Correspondence School children. In his ten years as principal at Auckland's inner-city Decile One Newton Central School, from 1988 to 1998, he endeavoured to put into practice many of the ideas outlined in this book.

Tim writes poetry and, occasionally, gets it published. He was, for many years, an MC at Poetry Live — Auckland's long-running weekly poetry event. He has won several poetry slams, including Poetry Idol, Womad and Going West. He was part of 'The Best of the Best' event at the 2017 Auckland Writers Festival. The Poetry Gold Cup, from Burnie in north-west Tasmania, is a prized possession, as is the People's Choice Award from the Bellingen Literary Festival in rural New South Wales. He was delighted to be voted People's Choice at the 2019 Going West Festival.

A collection of Tim's poetry was published in 2018, under the title *Not as the Crow Flies*. He writes about everyday life: relationships, shopping, parking, love and loss. He believes that poetry should not be difficult and that it's okay if a poem makes people laugh.

Time for writing is happily compromised by being a grand-father, reading, cooking, gardening, golfing, ocean sailing, watching cricket, tending an ageing Grey Lynn villa ...

... and dreaming.